DIVERSE SHORTS

LITERATURE
TO PROMOTE
CRITICAL THINKING

hackney learning trust

EMC Publications

DIVERSE SHORTS

Acknowledgements

Texts selected by Andrew McCallum and James Wright

Written by Andrew McCallum (English and Media Centre) and James Wright (Hackney Learning Trust)

Cover and chapter title pages: Rebecca Scambler, www.rebeccascambler.com (Cover uses 'Wall Street Art in a Public Place, Brooklyn, New York' by Chris Barbalis on Unsplash)

Published by English and Media Centre, 18 Compton Terrace, London, N1 2UN

© English and Media Centre, 2018

ISBN: 9781906101510

Printed by Stephens and George Ltd

Thanks to the following publishers, agents, writers and image libraries for granting permission to reproduce copyright material.

Nineteen Eighty-Four by George Orwell (Copyright © George Orwell, 1949) by permission of Bill Hamilton as the Literary Executor of the Estate of the Late Sonia Brownell Orwell

MBA Literary Agents Limited for *Tender Earth* by Sita Brahmachari

Hodder and Stoughton for 'Loose Change' from *Six Stories and an Essay* by Andrea Levy

Oberon Books for *Another World: Losing Our Children to Islamic State* by © Gillian Slovo

Canongate Books for 'Brownies' from *Drinking Coffee Elsewhere* by ZZ Packer

Bloomsbury for *Refugee Boy* by Benjamin Zephaniah

From *Orangeboy* by Patrice Lawrence, first published in the UK by Hodder Children's Books, an imprint of Hachette Children's Books, Carmelite House, 50 Victoria Embankment, London imprint

Little, Brown Book Group for the permission to reproduce an extract from *Crongton Knights* by Alex Wheatle

Thanks to the Luithlen Agency for 'The Colour of Humanity' from *Here I Stand* ed. Amnesty (Walker Books) Copyright © 2016 Bali Rai

United Agents for 'My Polish Teacher's Tie' from *Ice Cream* © Helen Dunmore

Walker Books for 'May Malone' by © David Almond from *The Children's Hours* and *The Hate U Give* by © Angie Thomas

Bonnier Zaffre for permission to reproduce extracts from Benjamin Zephaniah's *Terror Kid*

Scholastic Limited for *Looking for JJ* © Anne Cassidy, reproduced with permission of the Licensor through PLSClear

Stories of Your Life and Others by Ted Chiang, published by Picador, reproduced with permission of the Licensor through PLSClear.

Welcome to Nowhere by Elizabeth Laird published by Pan Macmillan, reproduced with permission of the Licensor through PLSClear

Other images and texts reproduced are either creative commons, licensed for re-use or out of copyright.

Every effort has been made to trace and acknowledge copyright, but if accidental infringement has been made, we would welcome information to redress the situation.

CONTENTS

Guidance for Teachers	**4**
Introduction for Readers	**6**
Identity, Diversity and Community	**7**
Tender Earth, by Sita Brahmachari	8
The Colour of Humanity, by Bali Rai	16
My Polish Teacher's Tie, by Helen Dunmore	23
Liking What You See, by Ted Chiang	30
Tolerance, Rights and Respect	**37**
May Malone, by David Almond	38
Loose Change, by Andrea Levy	45
Brownies, by ZZ Packer	52
Justice, Change and Action	**71**
Terror Kid, by Benjamin Zephaniah	72
Looking for JJ, by Anne Cassidy	82
Orangeboy, by Patrice Lawrence	89
Every Man Dies Alone, by Hans Fallada	108
Democracy, Equality and Responsibility	**113**
Welcome to Nowhere, by Elizabeth Laird	114
Refugee Boy, by Benjamin Zephaniah	125
Another World, by Gillian Slovo	132
Power, Freedom and Control	**139**
The Hate U Give, by Angie Thomas	140
Crongton Knights, by Alex Wheatle	144
Nineteen Eighty-Four, by George Orwell	149
Critical Literacy Questions	**155**

© ENGLISH & MEDIA CENTRE, 2018

GUIDANCE FOR TEACHERS

The stories and activities in this collection are designed to promote critical thinking in secondary school students from 11-16. Suitable for English, Citizenship, PSHE and tutor time, it is arranged in five thematic sections, each of which cover key aspects of critical understanding.

Each section moves from what we consider to be the least to the most challenging text. The texts in each share common themes and ideas, as indicated by the section headings, but often they could fit just as comfortably elsewhere in the book.

There are some weighty and challenging issues explored in the texts, so we recommend that you read in advance any that you intend to share with students. In particular, you might like to make note of the following:

- 'The Colour of Humanity' – based on a violent, real-life, racist assault.
- 'Brownies' – contains mild swearing and also racially offensive language (used in the context of exploring racism).
- *Orangeboy* – contains descriptions of drug-taking and one instance of swearing on page 97.
- *The Hate U Give* – one instance of mild swearing, plus violence.

The stories do not have to be read sequentially and it is also possible to compare stories across sections. At the back of the book you will find a series of detailed critical literacy questions that you can use with any or all of the texts – and which you might also like to use elsewhere in the curriculum. You can find copies to print off by searching 'Diverse Shorts' at www.englishandmedia.co.uk/publications

The activities for each story are set out in the same way following a three-part structure:

- **Connecting to the topic** – unless stated, this is to be done *before reading* the story. It gives students the opportunity to learn a little about the topic they are about to explore further in the story, as well as to reflect on their own existing knowledge and that of their classmates.

- **Connecting to the story** – this provides students with the opportunity to explore an important aspect of the story *after reading*. Lots of the activities require students to draw on skills of empathy, for example by writing in the voice of a character, or of the writer.

- **Connecting to the real world** – also to be done *after reading*, these activities encourage students to place their reading in the context of the wider world around them and, at times, to reflect on how the story has changed their understanding in some way.

DIVERSE SHORTS

DIVERSE SHORTS

LITERATURE
TO PROMOTE
CRITICAL THINKING

© ENGLISH & MEDIA CENTRE, 2018

INTRODUCTION FOR READERS

Dear Reader,

Welcome to *Diverse Shorts*, a very exciting publication for two reasons.

First, and foremost, it will introduce you to great writing in the form of short stories and novel extracts. We hope it will encourage you to read the work of the writers further and to seek out others who explore similar themes.

Second, it is designed to make you think critically. This doesn't mean we want you to think negatively; rather, it means we want you to think deeply about what you are reading, asking important questions about why it is written in particular ways, what it is trying to say, and what it might mean to different groups of people. Critical thinking is a key skill as you navigate your way through the modern world. You can apply ways of reading critically that you meet when looking at literature to just about any other text – be it serious or light, online or off, written or visual. So you'll be on your way to becoming an expert in spotting fake news, or working out the real agenda behind material that is not necessarily fake, but which is distinctly biased.

Each piece selected for this anthology deals with an important issue. That's why all of the sub-headings are so weighty. But you can be sure that whether you are reading a piece from 'Identity, Diversity and Community' or 'Power, Freedom and Control', the story comes first. And, as should be the case with a critical thinking approach to literature, your opinions about what you read matter most. The selections are designed to make you think, not to tell you what to think. To help you with this there is a series of 'critical literacy questions' at the back of the book, which carefully take you through the kinds of things you might ask of a piece of writing when exploring it critically.

The stories should appeal to you whatever your age. Some are more challenging than others, though, so the most straightforward appear at the start of each section. Several also deal with issues that your teacher might like to talk to you about carefully before you start your reading.

The questions have been chosen with secondary school students in mind, though, so they should be just up your street. And whether they are, or aren't, you should still be asking an important critical question: why do teachers think it is important for young people to read writing like this? If you can answer that question well, then the book has done its job!

Happy reading!

The English and Media Centre and the Hackney Learning Trust

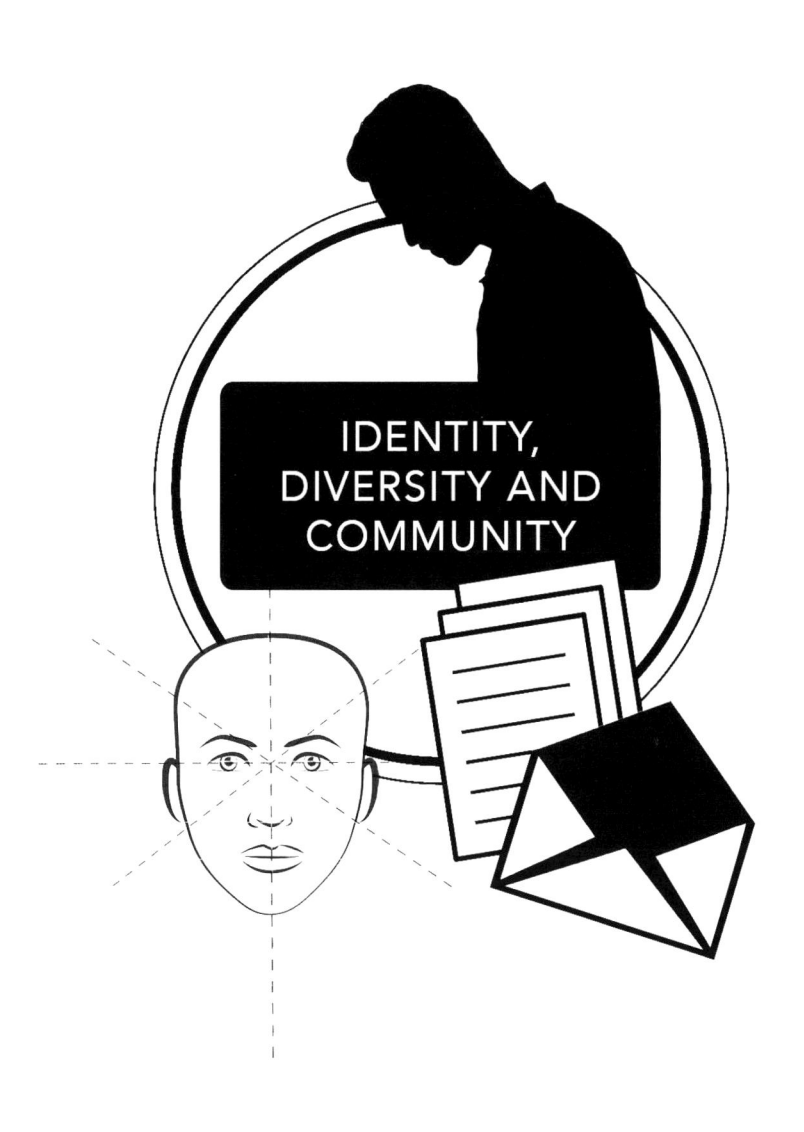

IDENTITY, DIVERSITY AND COMMUNITY

DIVERSE SHORTS

Tender Earth, by Sita Brahmachari

This extract from a novel focuses on tutor time for Laila during her first day at secondary school.

Connecting to the topic

- For each concept below, write a sentence or two to summarise what you think it means:
  - Identity
  - Diversity
  - Community.
- Why might a teacher think it's important for young people to learn about these concepts? Can you think of a reason for each?
- Listen to some of your ideas around the class.

Connecting to the story

- How realistic a picture does this chapter paint of a first day at school? Write down your own thoughts, focusing on the activities the pupils are doing, the way they behave, the teacher, and so on. You might like to think about what is really good about this lesson, or what you might like to change.
- Compare your thoughts round the class.

Connecting to the real world

- Individually complete a list like the one Laila and her classmates filled in. (So details of Name, Beliefs, Hobbies, Religion, Connected Lands, Favourite Subjects and Languages.)
- Share your lists around the class and discuss what it feels like to give out this information and to hear it from other people.
- What conclusions can you draw about the different backgrounds, identities and interests represented in your class?

IDENTITY, DIVERSITY AND COMMUNITY

TENDER EARTH

SITA BRAHMACHARI

I check down the list of names in my tutor group. Kez is definitely not on it. After what they said in our transition meeting, I still don't understand why we're not together. Unless… I just can't get the idea out of my head that Kez has somehow made this happen.

You could ask for two people you especially wanted to be with, but the only person I really cared about being with was Kez, so I didn't write down any other names. The only other person I know is a boy called Carlos. He only came to our primary in Year Six and he didn't speak much English then. It's incredible how good he is now though. I think he's Spanish, but I'm not sure. I don't know him that well.

Our tutor's called Mrs Latif. She tells us that she teaches Philosophy and Ethics and a subject called Citizenship, which I've heard Krish talking about. It was his best subject and he was really gutted they didn't do it as an exam. Mrs Latif is explaining why she chose 'Seven Dials' as our tutor-group name:

'Always so many different pathways to explore from the same starting point, or roundabout to be precise! Anyone know where Seven Dials is?'

I've been thinking that at secondary I should speak up more than I used to in primary, especially when I know the answer.

'Well, it's in Covent Garden,' Mrs Latif answers as no one puts their hand up.

Mrs Latif is tall and has a long, slim face with high cheekbones, dark eyes with thick lashes, perfectly sculpted eyebrows and a tiny diamond nose stud. Her lips are painted plum colour and her silvery headscarf is decorated at the side with diamond jewels. She wears a plain black dress and heavy silver jewellery. Her nails are painted the same plum colour as her lips. I love her shoes… they're like brogues but silver. It doesn't seem fair really. If students have to wear a uniform, why don't teachers?

Mrs Latif says she's just started teaching here, and at her old school she taught Religious Education.

'So you will be my philosophy ambassadors here!' she says.

DIVERSE SHORTS

Above the whiteboard she has a sign mounted on bright blue card,

> This school welcomes
> believers of all religions and none

I read it over a few times. I think it's a good thing she's written it up there on the wall so everyone knows, because when I watch the news lots of the things in the world where people fight with each other seem to have something to do with what religion they do or don't belong to; what they believe or don't. Mrs Latif takes her black marker pen and makes columns on the board under the headings:

| Name | Hobbies | Connected Lands | Languages |
| Beliefs | Religion | Favourite Subjects | |

I didn't think tutor time would be about stuff like this. Mrs Latif goes around the class taking the electronic register. She does it as fast as she can.

'Now. I thought we could start by getting to know a few things about each other! In a minute I'd like you to walk around the class with your notebooks, asking each other questions. I've put a few suggested headings up here to get you started –' she taps the board – 'but you can add whatever categories you like. We're just making a start at getting to know each other. Try to fill in as much as possible for as many people as possible in the time that we've got. In the next few weeks everyone will have met everyone else. Any questions?'

A girl sitting behind me puts her hand up.

'Is belief the same as religion?' she asks.

'This is exactly the sort of question I was hoping for... what's your name?'

'Pari.'

'Hi, Pari.' Mrs Latif thinks carefully before she answers. 'No, actually – I don't think they're the same. They're connected though. It's complicated, but that's the kind of thing we can debate in tutor time. You can also keep an eye out for any news that can feed into our discussions.'

'Excuse me? What does Connected Lands mean?' Carlos asks.

'Make a guess!'

'I'm from Spain, but my family live all over the world...'

IDENTITY, DIVERSITY AND COMMUNITY

'Where?' Mrs Latif asks.

'Well, my uncle's from Cuba. I have relatives in Mexico, France and Spain, America and Canada.'

'You've got it! But, like I said, you don't have to stick to my categories; they're just to get you started. Come on then! See how many people you can meet and how much of the globe we can span in the next few minutes.'

The room gradually fills with noise.

The first person I meet is someone called Stella. She says she doesn't see why we should be talking about 'personal stuff' on our first day at school, and when I talk to her the only question she will answer is her name: Stella Hetherington.

'What's it got to do with her or anyone else what I believe in?' Stella asks.

I don't think Stella realises that Mrs Latif is standing right behind us.

'The thing about secondary school, Stella, is that it can open the door to a whole other world you never knew anything about, *if* you're willing to step through.'

'Like we need any more doors open? I know where I'm from!' Stella mumbles under her breath.

Mrs Latif ignores her.

I tell Stella my name and move on because her lips are sealed and it's just getting embarrassing.

The next person I talk to is the girl called Pari who asked the question about belief. She shows me what she's written in her book under the categories.

Name:	Pari Pashaei
Languages:	English and Arabic
Hobbies:	Athletics and Reading
Connected Lands:	Iraq/UK
Beliefs:	Fairness, Justice, Human Rights
Religion:	Islam
Favourite Subjects:	History

She peers at my book. 'Your religion bit looks a bit complicated!' She laughs, reading over my shoulder.

'It is kind of hard for me to fill in.' I shrug. 'Maybe I haven't done it right.'

DIVERSE SHORTS

Name:	Laila Levenson
Languages:	English
Hobbies:	??? Dance?
Connected Lands:	India, Poland, UK, America
Religion:	Hinduism, Christianity, Judaism All/None?
Favourite Subjects:	?? Not sure

'Do you believe in one of these religions then?' Pari asks.

I look at the sign above the whiteboard.

'I'd say none.'

'But you know about them, right?'

'Not really. Well, a bit... I mean some people in my family do.'

I wish I could sound a bit more convincing.

Pari looks at me like what I've just told her hasn't made anything any clearer. She points to my name, I think to move the conversation on.

'Your name sounds a bit like my mum's... she's Leyla.'

Mrs Latif holds her hand in the air and counts down her fingers from eleven to one. Everyone's staring at her by the time she's done. She does actually have eleven fingers!

She holds her left hand in the air for us to all have a proper look.

'Introducing my baby finger!' she says, wiggling her little finger – and the baby offshoot wiggles too.

'Anyone else got an extra digit on their fingers or toes?'

No one puts their hand up.

'Well, there isn't another teacher in this school who'll do that countdown from eleven to one, so you've got one more count to be quiet... but don't test that extra digit! It's fiercer than it looks!' Mrs Latif jokes and everyone bursts out laughing – but she quickly does the countdown again and starts to look really mock-fierce as she gets to her sixth finger.

'Now let's just have a quick go round of what we've found out about each other in that short time.'

She writes the title: 'Seven Dials Harvest – Day One' on the board.

IDENTITY, DIVERSITY AND COMMUNITY

'How many languages have we got listed? Mr Keegan, our Head of Languages, will be interested in this. Only give me a new one if it hasn't been said before!' Mrs Latif starts going around the class and adding to the lists. People are from all different religions too:

Quaker, Islam, Christianity, Judaism, Sikhism, Catholicism, Jehovah's Witness, Hinduism... I can't believe how long each category goes on for – especially 'Connected Lands' and 'Languages'.

When we've pooled it all together, there are fifty-two different countries this class is connected to.

'How many countries are there in the world then?' a girl I just talked to asks.

I look down at my list. Her name's Milena, and her family's from Bulgaria.

'Debatable. One hundred and ninety-five or six?'

Milena whistles.

'But of course borders between countries do shift over time,' Mrs Latif answers, 'and not often peacefully.'

When she says this she puckers her lips like she's thinking of saying something else, and then she makes a popping sound with them as if to bring herself back to what she's doing.

Mrs Latif circles a language on the board called 'Lingala'. 'Who does this belong to?' She scans the class.

A girl I haven't met yet puts her hand up really shyly.

'Ah, Carmel!' Mrs Latif smiles encouragingly at the girl as she tells us that her parents are from Cameroon.

'Millions of people speak it,' she says, looking down at her desk.

I think she's a bit embarrassed. I know how she feels. I hate it when teachers spring questions on you that you weren't planning to answer.

'It sounds like a song... Lin-ga-La!' Mrs Latif almost sings the word and makes Carmel smile. And even though she does still look embarrassed, she seems kind of happy too.

Stella puts her hand up.

'I speak Italian and my grandpa on my mum's side speaks Cornish – does that count too?' she asks.

Mrs Latif adds 'Cornish' to the list of languages.

'I'd love to hear some Cornish. Do you speak it?'

Stella shakes her head.

'Could you ask your grandad to teach you some and then we can *all* learn a bit? And yes, Stella, it counts. It all counts.' Mrs Latif looks at her watch. 'Now hand your notes in and tomorrow I'll write up the lists in more detail. This is just the beginning of our map of Seven Dials… It's been useful to have this double lesson so we could make a good start, but it's still just a sketch at the moment and we'll be filling in more detail every day.'

'Do we have the same tutor *all* the way up the school?' Stella calls out, screwing up her nose.

'That's how it's organised in this school.' Mrs Latif smiles at Stella, who kicks against the back of the chair in front of her. 'I think it's a real opportunity for us all to grow up together!'

I'm sure Mrs Latif notices the look on Stella's face, but she focuses on the back of the classroom like she hasn't seen.

'Now, we'll gradually go over the rules over the next few weeks, but I should tell you all straight away that I've got one rule in this classroom that I will not tolerate being broken.'

She looks deadly serious for a moment, then her mouth springs into a dazzling smile. How does she make her lipstick stay on so perfectly? She takes her green marker and writes something on the board that I can't see until she's finished.

'No matter what else is happening outside of here, in the wider world, this is what I expect in my classroom…'

MUTUAL RESPECT

She underlines the words three times. 'Everyone know what 'mutual' means?' she asks, scanning the room for an answer and letting her gaze rest on Stella for the tiniest second.

A few people murmur the answer.

'Each other! That's right. Now, I'm going to send you on your way with my ethical question of the term… always a good one to get people going, I find! It seems that there's a lot of talk about 'truth' at the moment. Apparently there's something called 'post-truth' – a term that's officially in the dictionary – so I think we do need to look into it. When we say something's *post*-something, what do we mean?'

IDENTITY, DIVERSITY AND COMMUNITY

She writes examples on the board.

> Post-Modern
>
> Post-Natal
>
> Post-Script
>
> Post-Truth

'After,' Milena calls out.

'So what comes after truth?' Mrs Latif raises her eyebrows and shakes her head.

I'm not sure if she's actually asking us or whether she's just putting the question out there.

She turns back to the whiteboard. 'Who knows? But I always think a good way to examine something is to look at its opposite. The opposite of truth is...'

She doesn't turn around and a few people including Pari call out, 'Lie.'

Mrs Latif nods as she writes two questions on the whiteboard. 'This could be viewed as the same question, but it sometimes helps to play around with an idea. To turn it on its head.'

> Is it *always* wrong to lie?
>
> Is it *always* right to tell the truth?

'So, Seven Dials, that's tutor time over! No easy questions, no easy answers! Exercise your minds – that's the most important thing. Off you go now to your first lessons.'

Is it always *wrong to lie?*

Is it always *right to tell the truth?*

Maybe I should just call Mira and tell her I opened her letter.

DIVERSE SHORTS

The Colour of Humanity, by Bali Rai

Connecting to the topic

The title of this story gives you a clue about what it is going to be about. Without giving too much away, it explores issues around judging people based on the colour of their skin.

- As a whole class discuss stories you know already, from books, TV, film, and so on, which explore the same issues.

- What do these stories have in common? For example, are they generally positive and uplifting, or more depressing? Are they realistic and everyday, or do they focus on unusual, one-off events?

Connecting to the story

The writer, Bali Rai, wrote in a footnote to this story, 'I believe that empathy is the first line of defence against hatred'. Empathy is the ability to share and understand the feelings of another.

- Re-read the story with a partner and identify five points in the story when the narrator shows empathy. This could be something he does, or simply the way that he says something.

- Share your examples as a class and discuss what message you think the writer is trying to get across.

Connecting to real life

- In pairs, come up with a list of 10 things that everyone has in common, regardless of the colour of their skin. Try to be as imaginative as possible with your suggestions (e.g. we all have music in our souls).

- Listen to different ideas around the class.

IDENTITY, DIVERSITY AND COMMUNITY

THE COLOUR OF HUMANITY

BALI RAI

If I could speak to you again, I would remind you about the park that we played in. Those multi-coloured rubber tiles in the kids' play area, surrounded by bark chips that would get stuck in our shoes. The fence around the perimeter that kept danger away, and us feeling safe. I loved the swings but you were a roundabout fan. We still enjoyed it the same, though, didn't we? I can see your mum sharing gossip with mine, the two of them watching over us, proud and happy.

Remember the other kids from the neighbourhood? My cousins Michael and Joseph, Ruby Khan and Mia McCullough – and so many others whose names I've forgotten. The laughter and the fun, and the sun shining over the holidays. Going home tired and sweaty, our fingers sticky from melted ice lollies. It's like a different world now, isn't it? Just a dream that we once shared. Maybe you saw something else in those images, something that didn't include me. Or was it later that we stopped being the same? I guess I'll never know.

I'd offer you my food, if I could see you again, like I did every time you came for tea. Fish fingers and chips, and those tinned peas that my mum always kept in the cupboard. You loved putting tomato ketchup on yours – smothering everything in it until your food was floating in a bloody lake. You'd get your fork and smear a chip around the plate, making patterns in the sauce. Call it painting. Mum used to say you'd become one of them modern artists, like that man who cut the shark in half, or that Banksy fella. Something avant-garde, she said, and we didn't know what she meant – looked it up on my laptop.

You never took my food though, did you? I didn't like ketchup. I used to dollop mayonnaise on my plate, and you'd pull that face, like there was a really bad smell in the room. Mayo, you'd say, sounding just like your nan. *Ma-yo? How can you eat that muck?* you'd ask. *It looks like sick.* And I'd just grin, spear a chip and wave it at you. Ketchup and mayo – that's who we were. Only, underneath the sauce, our food was the same. *We* were different, too – came out of different bottles, your mum said – but it didn't mean anything at all. We were always the same. Always.

DIVERSE SHORTS

In Year Six I'd help you with your maths. Mrs Cooper's class – remember it? Every bit of every wall covered in paintings and stories, and maps and times tables. That big chart about grammar and punctuation, and *were* versus *we're*, and all that stuff. Gold and silver stars next to every pupil's name, and the timeline of major world events. The yellow and red chairs that we'd scrape across the floor just to annoy Mrs Cooper. The tiny tables, the bookshelves, and the corner where Jordan O'Connor puked after eating all those chocolates, after we egged him on. Mia started crying because Jordan was her dad's cousin on his mother's side. She didn't talk to us again, until you bought her a bag of sweets with your birthday money.

You'd say you didn't do maths, called it the devil's language once. Mrs Cooper touched her crucifix necklace and called you a wicked child. But you didn't care, because maths was useless. You'd tap your calculator and say, *I've got this, haven't I?* Then you'd look over at my answers, and I'd let you see. Just you and no one else. I was your brother from another mother, you said. And I never cared about you copying my work, because I wanted to help you. I *liked* helping you. You were my best mate, and that's what friends are supposed to do.

If we could meet up again, I'd take you back to Nando's, like that first time we went. You and me, and our mums, walking through town without a care in the world, even though it was cold and wet, and the football fans were going to the match. My mum ordering us to cover our ears, and your mum telling those lads off for swearing around us. It was a big treat, remember? We'd finished Year Six and were on our way to big school. Money was tight but our mums had saved up, and we had chicken and chips, and that coleslaw that we ate out of the boxes.

I dared you to try the hot sauce, and you just laughed and said yeah. But when you tried it, your face went red and you began to cough. You grabbed every drink on the table and downed them, one after the other. Our mums were nearly crying with laughter and you ran off to the toilet.

And all the time I didn't even smile, because I felt so guilty, like I'd hurt you, and I wanted to say sorry but never did. When you came back, you were angry and wouldn't speak to me until your mum told you to grow up. I can't help thinking perhaps that was the moment – because you were never the same after that.

I would ask you about Year Seven, if I could, and those first few weeks, when you found new people to chill with. I'd point at Mia and Ruby, and Michael and Joseph, and even Jordan O'Connor, and say, what's the deal with that Brandon lad and his dodgy mates? At first you were fine, told me you had new friends, nothing special. Just natural to meet other people, you said. And we were together anyway, in the same form, the same classes – all of that.

IDENTITY, DIVERSITY AND COMMUNITY

So when your Uncle Tommy took us to the football, it still felt the same. Like we were still brothers. You had your blue shirt and I was wearing red, but that didn't matter. It was just football. We went to the chippy, and then stood outside the pub while your uncle and his mates had a few pints and talked about the game. Remember the banter that day? We felt like proper grown-up men, not the kids we were. Like we were part of something. And even though your side lost, you were still OK with it, and we had dodgy burgers on the way home – still the ketchup and mayo twins.

But that was the last time, I reckon. The last time we were brothers. The last time it didn't matter that we hadn't come from the same bottle. That we weren't the same on the outside.

See, if I could ask, I'd point to the books. You know the ones that I borrowed from school, and the local library in the neighbourhood centre. I'd ask why reading made me a geek, because that's what you started calling me. Was it so bad that I wanted to be something, to make my life better? How come you couldn't understand that?

Then I'd ask why you stopped knocking at my door, and why, when I walked to the shops, you'd be sitting there with Brandon and the others, acting all hard, like some wannabe gangster. Sharing cigarettes, thinking you were rude boys, or blagging cans of lager from some older cousin or whoever. Those girls you had with you, too – all wearing more make-up than clothes, and swearing like old men at the football.

I remember you looking to Brandon every time you spoke to me, like the two of you shared some private joke. Brandon grinning on the sly, or one of his boys pulling a face.

The big change happened in Year Nine, didn't it? It was that night in McDonald's. Michael and me had asked Ruby and Mia to come with us. We were on the bench outside, drinking Cokes, remember? You came up with Brandon and two other lads, and started causing trouble. The Asian security guard told you to leave, and you called him a *paki*, and the four of us couldn't believe it. You just said it, right out loud, like it was a regular insult – just banter, nothing more. Even though Ruby's dad was from Pakistan, and you knew it would upset her. You looked right at her and grinned.

When I saw you the next day, you told me I was boring and that I should go out more, and forget about school. Said I couldn't take a joke, and that I couldn't be properly English if I hung around with Muslims. We were at war, you said, and people had to stand up for what was right. All I remember thinking was that Ruby was just like us, just fish fingers smothered in a different sauce. And that your voice sounded familiar but the words you spoke weren't yours. They belonged to someone else, someone vicious and nasty and full of hate.

I'd rave about the basketball court at school if you were with me now. I loved that place; it was like a second home. I spent every spare second there, honing my game, shooting from every angle, over and over again. The ping of the ball as it bounced off the concrete, with Mia watching from the side-lines, eating those sour cherry sweets that she loved. That was where it happened, the first time – if you're interested. When she told me that she liked me, and we went over to the Spar and I got her more of those sweets. Walking home with my basketball in one hand and her hand in the other.

I remember you and that Brandon lad, standing by the railings, watching me practise. I remember wondering if you wanted a game – to maybe play some one-on-one. I remember you watching Mia, watching me. I didn't think it meant anything.

But you got worse, didn't you? Acted like I'd done something to let you down. As though Mia and I owed you an explanation because we were together. All that time, I thought it was envy. But you'd never once talked about Mia that way, or told me that you liked her. You used to talk about other girls, and those celebrity women off the Internet. I must have been blind or stupid, or a bit of both, to think it was jealousy that made you cut the bonds between us. I must have been so naive, so caught up in the lie that we'd be brothers for ever. That nothing could divide us.

So, I think about the bus stop most of all. It's natural, I guess, because that was where it all happened. I think about the warm evening sunshine on my face. I think about the glow that holding hands with Mia gave me, as my cousin Michael teased us for being loved-up. We were waiting for the number 27 bus to take us into town, and talking about the film we'd decided to watch. Just three friends having a laugh. Three regular English teenagers, loving life and living it. No pressures, no school, no problems other than deciding which screening to go to, and which snacks to buy when we got there.

I think about that scene as the trailer from a longer film, and it isn't supposed to end there. There were so many more scenes to play out over the years. So many more happy afternoons, and mild summer evenings…

You came out of the pub over the road, remember? You and Brandon, and that thug with the beige Stone Island jacket. I never knew his name, just knew the type – shaven head, tattoos and that snarl when he saw me holding Mia's hand. That word that every one of my ancestors has heard since they were taken from their homeland. Since they ended up in this country. That word that makes us

IDENTITY, DIVERSITY AND COMMUNITY

something less than people, that belittles our humanity, our experiences, our hopes and our dreams, until all we are is a colour.

What were you thinking when it started, I wonder? Where did that hate take root? You looked right through us, and Mia and Michael fled. They ran back through the park, screaming at me to follow them. But I didn't move, because when I saw you coming I saw my friend, my brother, the lad I'd known since we'd both worn nappies.

Brandon had the first pop – two punches to my face. I had to kneel, to try and regain my thoughts, my breath. I didn't cry then – I was too shocked, too angry. Then I saw your boot; just for a split second but I knew it was yours. I fell on my side, remember? Lay there, looking up at that hazy blue sky through tears, wondering where it had all gone wrong. When I went from being your brother to being someone with less right to walk down the street than you.

The thug, he pulled that thing from his jacket – I don't even know what it was. I just felt the crack and then all that pain. My skull felt like it was on fire. I knew then that it was over, and I tried to turn my head towards you. I managed to catch your eyes, and I *know* you remember that. Your face was twisted, contorted in rage, but your eyes were the same, brother. The same as when we ate fish fingers as the ketchup and mayo twins, the same as when we shared jokes and kicked footballs, and ran around the streets together. When what I was on the outside meant nothing to you.

So, let me ask you something else. Sitting in that cell, breathing in your own stink and that of others, what do you reflect on? Do you remember the playground, and the friends we had, and all those simple, naive childhood days? Do you find yourself back at the football, singing the songs and enjoying the banter? Does your mind play tricks on you at night? Does it take you back to the times when nothing but love and laughter and having fun mattered?

I lost so much that day. I lost my girl, and my family. I lost my chance to live a life the way it should be lived. I lost my dreams, my hopes. I wanted to be a lawyer. I wanted to have children of my own, and watch my mum play with them as she once did with me. I had the right to those things, just like anyone else. I had the right to become what I should have become. But ignorance and hate took that away. You took that away.

Only, you threw away as much of your own life as mine. The two of us, we're still the same, aren't we? Me in this bed, looking at nothing, feeling nothing, just a shell of the human I once was. You in that cell, your freedom gone, your life thrown away.

DIVERSE SHORTS

Neither of us is free, neither of us has a life. Mine ended that evening. I'll never get up again, never move on. I'll never walk or talk, or be able to hug my mum and tell her things will be OK. But your life is over too. Your life is rotting slowly away in there – and even though you can walk, and you can talk, you aren't *free*, are you?

Tell me, when you sit and stare at those walls, do you ever ask yourself when it happened, exactly where the turning point was? What caused the change?

See, humanity has no colour, brother. It did not start with a colour; it will not end with one. Remember all those lessons we were taught – to share, to accept, to respect the other? Well, when did I change for you, my friend?

When did you negate almost every aspect of my humanity until all you had left was my skin tone?

When did I stop being human first and start being black?

> Bali Rai comments:
>
> My story is inspired by the tragic death of Liverpool teenager Anthony Walker in 2005, at the hands of racists. It is a re-imagination of the facts, an attempt to explore the emotions of the victim. I believe that empathy is the first line of defence against hatred and I want to live in a world where race matters less than eye colour. We are a long way off, but every step we take towards that goal is precious and welcome. My story is designed to make you think about what makes us human. I hope that it does.

IDENTITY, DIVERSITY AND COMMUNITY

My Polish Teacher's Tie, by Helen Dunmore

Connecting to the topic

We often think of identity as being closely linked to our background and our personal preferences. But, once you are an adult, it is also often linked to your job.

- Discuss as a class the ways in which some jobs are valued more than others. Discuss whether or not this is fair. Do attitudes towards people's jobs suggest prejudices to do with particular activities, levels of wealth, and so on?

- In pairs, select three jobs that you think society does not traditionally value enough. Present back to the class why you think these jobs should be given more status.

Connecting to the story

- With a partner discuss how this story could be rewritten from the Polish teacher, Stefan's, perspective.

- On your own, write two or three paragraphs of the story in Stefan's voice.

Connecting to real life

Here are a list of different jobs selected at random: *teacher, cleaner, football manager, lorry driver, actor, soldier, doctor, fitness instructor, receptionist, gardener, farmer, nurse, builder, call-centre operator, florist.*

- In small groups try to find connections between as many of these as possible. See if you can manage this with unlikely pairings, e.g. fitness instructor and lorry driver: both have an interest in the efficient use of energy.

- Share your ideas as a whole class and discuss why it is important to focus on what we have in common, as well as to recognise our differences.

DIVERSE SHORTS

MY POLISH TEACHER'S TIE

HELEN DUNMORE

I wear a uniform, blue overall and white cap with the school logo on it. Part-time catering staff, that's me, £3.89 per hour. I dish out tea and buns to the teachers twice a day, and I shovel chips on to the kids' trays at dinner-time. It's not a bad job. I like the kids.

The teachers pay for their tea and buns. It's one of those schemes teachers are good at. So much into a kitty, and that entitles them to cups of tea and buns for the rest of the term. Visitors pay, too, or it wouldn't be fair. Very keen on fairness, we are, here.

It was ten-forty-five when the Head got up to speak. He sees his staff together for ten minutes once a week, and as usual he had a pile of papers in front of him. I never listen to any of it as a rule, but as I was tipping up the teapot to drain I heard him mention Poland.

I am half-Polish. They don't know that here. My name's not Polish or anything. It was my mother, she came here after the war. I spoke Polish till I was six, Baby Polish full of rhymes Mum taught me. Then my father put a stop to it. 'You'll get her all mixed up, now she's going to school. What use is Polish ever going to be to her?' I can't speak it now. I've got a tape, a tape of me speaking Polish with Mum. I listen, and I think I'm going to understand what we're saying, and then I don't.

'... long-term aim is to arrange a teacher exchange – several Polish teachers are looking for penfriends in English schools, to improve their written English... so if you're interested, the information's all here...'

He smiled, wagging the papers, and raised his eyebrows. I wrung out a cloth and wiped my surfaces. I was thinking fast. Thirteen minutes before I was due downstairs.

The meeting broke up and the Head vanished in a knot of teachers wanting to talk to him. I lifted the counter-flap, tucked my hair under the cap, and walked across. Teachers are used to getting out of the way of catering staff without really seeing them.

IDENTITY, DIVERSITY AND COMMUNITY

'Excuse me,' I said, pushing forward, 'excuse me,' and they did. Then I was in front of the Head. 'Excuse me,' I said again, and he broke off what he was saying. I saw him thinking, *trouble*. The kids chucking chips again. He stitched a nice smile on his face and said, 'Oh, er – Mrs, er – Carter. Is there a problem?'

'No,' I said, 'I was just wondering, could I have that address?'

'Address?'

'The Polish one. You said there was a Polish teacher who wanted an English penfriend.'

'Oh. Ah, yes. Of course.' He paused, looking at me as if it might be a trick question. 'Is it for yourself?'

'I'd like to write to a Polish teacher.'

'Oh,' he said. 'Yes. Of course, Mrs Carter.'

I took the address and smiled at him.

When Steve's first letter came I saw he'd taken it for granted I was a teacher. The person he had in his head when he was writing to me was an English teacher, a real professional. This person earned more money than him and had travelled and seen places and done things he'd never been able to do. He was really called Stefan, but he said he was going to call himself Steve when he wrote to me.

Jade saw the letter. 'What's that, Mum?'

'Just a letter. You can have the stamp if you want.'

In the second letter Steve told me that he wrote poetry.

'I have started a small literary magazine in our department. If you want, I am happy to send you some of our work.'

I told him about Jade. I told him about the songs my mother taught me in Polish, the ones I used to know but I'd forgotten. I didn't write anything about my job. Let him think what he wanted to think. I wasn't lying.

The first poem he sent me was about a bird in a coal mine. He sent me the English translation. This bird flew down the main shaft and got lost in the tunnels underground, then it sang and sang until it died. Everyone heard it singing, but no one could find it. I liked that poem. It made me think maybe I'd been missing something, because I hadn't read any poetry since I left school. I wrote back, 'Send me the Polish, just so I can see it.' When the Polish came I tried it over in my head. It sounded a bit like the rhymes my mother used to sing.

DIVERSE SHORTS

At first we wrote every week, then it was twice. I used to write a bit every day then make myself wait until the middle of the week to send it. I wrote after Jade was in bed. Things would suddenly come to me. I'd write, *'Oh, Steve, I've just remembered...'*, or *'... Do you see what I mean, Steve, or does it sound funny?'* It made it seem more like talking to him when I used his name.

He wrote me another poem. It was about being half-Polish and half-English, and the things I'd told him about speaking Polish until I was six and then forgetting it all:

'Mother, I've lost the words you gave me. Call the police, tell them there's a reward... I'll do anything ...'

He was going to put it in the literary magazine, *'if you have no objection, Carla'*. That was the way he wrote, always very polite. I said it was fine by me.

One day the Head stopped me and said, 'Did you ever write to that chap? The Polish teacher?'

'Yes,' I said. Nothing more. Let him think I'd written once then not bothered. Luckily, Mrs Callendar came up to talk about OFSTED.

'Ah, yes, OFSTED. Speaking of visitors,' said the Head, raising his voice the way he does so that one minute he's talking to you and the next it's a public announcement, 'I have news of progress on the Polish teachers' exchange. A teacher will be coming over from Katowice next month. His name is Stefan Jeziorny, and he will be staying with Mrs Kenward. We're most grateful to you for your hospitality, Valerie.'

Mrs Kenward flushed. The Head beamed at nobody. Stefan Jeziorny, I thought. I had clicked, even though I was so used to thinking of him as Steve. Why hadn't he said he was coming?

* * *

I dropped Jade off to tea with her friend. There was a letter waiting when I got home. I tore it open and read it with my coat still on. There was a bit about my last letter, and poetry, and then the news.

'You will know from your school, Carla, that I will come to England. I am hoping to make many contacts for the future, for other teachers who will also come to English schools. I hope, Carla, that you will introduce me to your colleagues. I will stay with an English Family who offer accommodation.'

I felt terrible. He sounded different, not like Steve. Not just polite any more, but all stiff, and a bit hurt. He must have thought I'd known about his visit from

IDENTITY, DIVERSITY AND COMMUNITY

the other teachers, and I hadn't wanted to invite him to stay with me. But what was worse was that he was going to expect to meet me. Or not me, exactly, but the person he'd been writing to, who didn't really exist. *'I have been corresponding with a colleague of yours, Carla Carter,'* he'd say to the other teachers. Then he'd wait for someone to say, *'Yes, of course, Carla's here, she's expecting you.'*

Colleagues don't wear blue overalls and white caps and work for £3.89 an hour. Somebody'd remember me asking the Head for his address, and there'd be a whisper running all round, followed by a horrible silence. They'd all look round at the serving-hatch and there I'd be, the big teapot in my hand and a plate of buns in front of me. And Steve'd look too. He'd still be smiling, because that's what you do in a foreign place when you don't know what's going on.

He'd think I was trying to make a fool of him, making him believe I was a teacher. Me, Carla Carter, part-time catering assistant, writing to him about poetry.

I could be off sick. I could swap with Jeannie. She could do the teachers' breaks. Or I could say Jade was ill.

No. That wouldn't work. Steve had my name, and my address. I sat down and spread out his letter again, then I went to the drawer and got all his other letters. I'd never had letters like that before and I was never going to again, not after Steve knew who I really was.

I didn't write, and Steve didn't write again either. I couldn't decide if it was because he was hurt, or because he knew he'd be seeing me soon anyway. The fuss Valerie Kenward made about having him to stay, you'd think the Pope was coming for a fortnight. I never liked her. Always holding up the queue saying she's on a diet, and then taking the biggest bun.

'If you're that bothered,' I said, 'he can come and stay in my flat, with me and Jade.' But I said it to myself, in my head. I knew he'd want to be with the other teachers.

I couldn't stop looking for letters. And then there was the poetry book I'd bought. It seemed a shame to bin it. It might come in for Jade, I thought.

A week went by, eight days, ten. Each morning I woke up and I knew something was wrong before I could remember what it was. It got worse every day until I thought, *Sod it, I'm not going to worry any more.*

The next morning-break the buns were stale. Valerie Kenward poked them, one after another. 'We ought to get our money back,' she said. But she still took one, and waited while I filled the teapot from the urn.

'How's it going?' Susie Douglas asked her.

27

'*Hard work!*' stage-whispered Valerie, rolling her eyes.

'He's not got much conversation, then?'

'Are you joking? All he wants to talk about is poetry. It's hell for the kids, he doesn't mean to be funny but they can't keep a straight face. It's the way he talks. Philippa had to leave the room at supper-time, and I can't say I blame her.'

You wouldn't, I thought. If ever anyone brought up their kids to be pleased with themselves, it's Valerie Kenward.

'And even when it's quite a well-known writer like Shakespeare or Shelley, you can't make out what he's on about. It's the accent.'

'He is Polish. I mean, how many Polish poets could you pronounce?' asked Susie.

'And his ties!' went on Valerie. 'You've never seen anything like them.'

I looked past both of them. I'd have noticed him before, if I hadn't been so busy. He was sitting stiffly upright, smiling in the way people smile when they don't quite understand what's going on. The Head was wagging a sheaf of papers in front of him, and talking very loudly, as if he was deaf. Steve. Stefan Jeziorny. He was wearing a brown suit with padded shoulders. It looked too big for him. His tie was wider than normal ties, and it was red with bold green squiggles on it. It was a terribly hopeful tie. His shoes had a fantastic shine on them. His face looked much too open, much too alive, as if a child Jade's age had got into an adult's body.

'Isn't that tea made *yet*?' asked Valerie.

I looked at her. 'No,' I said. 'It's not. Excuse me,' and I lifted the counter-flap and ducked past her while her mouth was still open. I walked up to where Steve was sitting. He looked round at me the way a child does when he doesn't know anyone at a party, hoping for rescue.

'Hello,' I said. He jumped up, held out his hand. 'How do you do?' he asked, as if he really wanted to know. I took his hand. It was sweaty, as I'd known it would be. He was tense as a guitar string.

'I'm Carla,' I said.

'Carla?' He couldn't hide anything. I saw it all swim in his eyes. Surprise. Uncertainty. What was he going to do? And then I saw it. Pleasure. A smile lit in his eyes and ran to his mouth.

'Carla! You are Carla Carter. My penfriend.'

'Yes.' Then he did something I still can't quite believe. He stood there holding on to my hand right in the middle of the staffroom, his big bright tie blazing, and

IDENTITY, DIVERSITY AND COMMUNITY

he sang a song I knew. It went through me like a knife through butter. A Polish song. I knew it, I knew it. I knew the words and the tune. It was one of the songs my mother used to sing to me. I felt my lips move. There were words in my mouth, words I didn't understand. And then I was singing, stumbling after him all the way to the end of the verse.

'Good heavens. How very remarkable. I didn't realise you were Polish, Mrs... er...' said the Head as he bumbled round us flapping his papers.

'Nor did I,' I said. But I wasn't going to waste time on the Head. I wanted to talk about poetry. I smiled at Steve. His red tie with its bold green squiggles was much too wide and much too bright. It was a flag from another country, a better country than the ones either of us lived in. 'I like your tie,' I said.

DIVERSE SHORTS

Liking What You See, by Ted Chiang

Connecting to the topic

This extract is from the start of a science-fiction story that imagines a future world in which people are given a treatment which brings about 'calliagnosia' ('calli' for short). This is a condition in which it is impossible to detect beauty or ugliness in a person's face. It is used to eliminate 'lookism' – a word the story uses to describe discriminating against people based on their looks.

- As a class, discuss whether schools should tackle 'lookism' in the same way that they also tackle sexism, racism, homophobia, and so on.

Connecting to the story

You have only been given the start of what is quite a long short story, which draws on lots of different voices as it develops.

- In twos or threes, discuss how you think the story will continue, how it will end, and what message it is likely to put across to its readers. You should focus, in particular, on the character of Tamera Lyons.
- Write a short extract in the voice of Tamera Lyons from later on in the story.

Connecting to real life

- In small groups, discuss your thoughts about these two statements:

> It is unacceptable to comment negatively on someone's appearance.

> Judging people based on what they look like is part of human nature.

- Open up your discussion to the whole class.

IDENTITY, DIVERSITY AND COMMUNITY

LIKING WHAT YOU SEE: A DOCUMENTARY

TED CHIANG

'Beauty is the promise of happiness.'
- Stendhal

Tamera Lyons, first-year student at Pembleton:

I can't believe it. I visited the campus last year, and I didn't hear a word about this. Now I get here and it turns out people want to make calli a requirement. One of the things I was looking forward to about college was getting rid of this, you know, so I could be like everybody else. If I'd known there was even a chance I'd have to keep it, I probably would have picked another college. I feel like I've been scammed.

I turn eighteen next week, and I'm getting my calli turned off that day. If they vote to make it a requirement I don't know what I'll do; maybe I'll transfer, I don't know. Right now I feel like going up to people and telling them, 'Vote no.' There's probably some campaign I can work for.

Maria deSouza, third-year student, President of the Students for Equality Everywhere (SEE):

Our goal is very simple. Pembleton University has a Code of Ethical Conduct, one that was created by the students themselves, and that all incoming students agree to follow when they enrol. The initiative that we've sponsored would add a provision to the code, requiring students to adopt calliagnosia as long as they're enrolled.

What prompted us to do this now was the release of a spex version of Visage. That's the software that, when you look at people through your spex, shows you what they'd look like with cosmetic surgery. It became a form of entertainment among a certain crowd, and a lot of college students found it offensive. When people started talking about it as a symptom of a deeper societal problem, we thought the timing was right for us to sponsor this initiative.

The deeper societal problem is lookism. For decades people've been willing to talk about racism and sexism, but they're still reluctant to talk about lookism. Yet this prejudice against unattractive people is incredibly pervasive. People do it without even being taught by anyone, which is bad enough, but instead of combating this tendency, modern society actively reinforces it.

Educating people, raising their awareness about this issue, all of that is essential, but it's not enough. That's where technology comes in. Think of calliagnosia as a kind of assisted maturity. It lets you do what you know you should: ignore the surface, so you can look deeper.

We think it's time to bring calli into the mainstream. So far the calli movement has been a minor presence on college campuses, just another one of the special-interest causes. But Pembleton isn't like other colleges, and I think the students here are ready for calli. If the initiative succeeds here, we'll be setting an example for other colleges, and ultimately, society as a whole.

Joseph Weingartner, neurologist:

The condition is what we call an associative agnosia, rather than an apperceptive one. That means it doesn't interfere with one's visual perception, only with the ability to recognise what one sees. A calliagnosic perceives faces perfectly well; he or she can tell the difference between a pointed chin and a receding one, a straight nose and a crooked one, clear skin and blemished skin. He or she simply doesn't experience any aesthetic reaction[1] to those differences.

Calliagnosia is possible because of the existence of certain neural pathways in the brain. All animals have criteria for evaluating the reproductive potential of prospective mates, and they've evolved neural 'circuitry' to recognise those criteria. Human social interaction is centred around our faces, so our circuitry is most finely attuned to how a person's reproductive potential is manifested in his or her face. You experience the operation of that circuitry as the feeling that a person is beautiful, or ugly, or somewhere in between. By blocking the neural pathways dedicated to evaluating those features, we can induce calliagnosia.

Given how much fashions change, some people find it hard to imagine that there are absolute markers of a beautiful face. But it turns out that when people of different cultures are asked to rank photos of faces for attractiveness, some very

---

1   A response based on looks and ideas of beauty.

IDENTITY, DIVERSITY AND COMMUNITY

clear patterns emerge across the board. Even very young infants show the same preference for certain faces. This lets us identify certain traits that are common to everyone's idea of a beautiful face.

Probably the most obvious one is clear skin. It is the equivalent of a bright plumage in birds or a shiny coat of fur in other mammals. Good skin is the single best indicator of youth and health, and it's valued in every culture. Acne may not be serious, but it *looks* like more serious diseases and that's why we find it disagreeable.

Another trait is symmetry; we may not be conscious of millimetre differences between someone's left and right sides, but measurements reveal that individuals rated as most attractive are also the most symmetrical. And while symmetry is what our genes always aim for, it's very difficult to achieve in developmental terms; any environmental stressor – like poor nutrition, disease, parasites – tends to result in asymmetry during growth. Symmetry implies resistance to such stressors.

Other traits have to do with facial proportions. We tend to be attracted to facial proportions that are close to the population mean. That obviously depends on the population you're part of, but being near the mean usually indicates genetic health. The only departures from the mean that people consistently find attractive are ones caused by sex hormones, which suggest good reproductive potential.

Basically, calliagnosia is a lack of response to these traits; nothing more. Calliagnosics are *not* blind to fashion or cultural standards of beauty. If black lipstick is all the rage, calliagnosia won't make you forget it, although you might not notice the difference between pretty faces and plain faces wearing that lipstick. If everyone around you sneers at people with broad noses, you'll pick up on that.

So calliagnosia by itself can't eliminate appearance-based discrimination. What it does, in a sense, is even up the odds; it takes away the innate predisposition, the tendency for such discrimination to arise in the first place. That way, if you want to teach people to ignore appearances, you won't be facing an uphill battle. Ideally you'd start with an environment where everyone's adopted calliagnosia, and then socialise them to not value appearances.

Tamera Lyons:
People here have been asking me what it was like going to Saybrook, growing up with calli. To be honest, it's not a big deal when you're young; you know, like they say, whatever you grew up with seems normal to you. We knew that there was something that other people could see that we couldn't, but it was just something we were curious about.

For instance, my friends and I used to watch movies and try to figure out who was really good-looking and who wasn't. We'd say we could tell, but we couldn't really, not by looking at their faces. We were just going by who was the main character and who was the friend; you always knew the main character was better-looking than the friend. It's not true a hundred percent of the time, but you could usually tell if you were watching the kind of thing where the main character wouldn't be good-looking.

It's when you get older that it starts to bother you. If you hang out with people from other schools, you can feel weird because you have calli and they don't. It's not that anyone makes a big deal out of it, but it reminds you that there's something you can't see. And then you start having fights with your parents, because they're keeping you from seeing the real world. You never get anywhere with them, though.

Richard Hamill, founder of the Saybrook School:

Saybrook came about as an outgrowth of our housing cooperative. We had maybe two dozen families at the time, all trying to establish a community based on shared values. We were holding a meeting about the possibility of starting an alternative school for our kids, and one parent mentioned the problem of the media's influence on their kids. Everyone's teens were asking for cosmetic surgery so they could look like fashion models. The parents were doing their best, but you can't isolate your kids from the world; they live in an image-obsessed culture.

It was around the time the last legal challenges to calliagnosia were resolved, and we got to talking about it. We saw calli as an opportunity: What if we could live in an environment where people didn't judge each other on their appearance? What if we could raise our children in such an environment?

The school started out being just for the children of the families in the cooperative, but other calliagnosia schools began making the news, and before long people were asking if they could enrol their kids without joining the housing co-op. Eventually we set up Saybrook as a private school separate from the co-op, and one of its requirements was that parents adopt calliagnosia for as long as their kids were enrolled. Now a calliagnosia community has sprung up here, all because of the school.

Rachel Lyons:

Tamera's father and I gave the issue a lot of thought before we decided to enrol her there. We talked to people in the community, found we liked their approach to education, but really it was visiting the school that sold me.

IDENTITY, DIVERSITY AND COMMUNITY

Saybrook has a higher than normal number of students with facial abnormalities, like bone cancer, burns, congenital conditions. Their parents moved here to keep them from being ostracised by other kids, and it works. I remember when I first visited, I saw a class of twelve-year-olds voting for class president, and they elected this girl who had burn scars on one side of her face. She was wonderfully at ease with herself, she was popular among kids who probably would have ostracised her in any other school. And I thought, this is the kind of environment I want my daughter to grow up in.

Girls have always been told that their value is tied to their appearance; their accomplishments are always magnified if they're pretty and diminished if they're not. Even worse, some girls get the message that they can get through life relying on just their looks, and then they never develop their minds. I wanted to keep Tamera away from that sort of influence. Being pretty is fundamentally a passive quality; even when you work at it, you're working at being passive. I wanted Tamera to value herself in terms of what she could do, both with her mind and with her body, not in terms of how decorative she was. I didn't want her to be passive, and I'm pleased to say that she hasn't turned out that way.

Martin Lyons:

I don't mind if Tamera decides as an adult to get rid of calli. This was never about taking choices away from her. But there's more than enough stress involved in simply getting through adolescence; the peer pressure can crush you like a paper cup. Becoming preoccupied with how you look is just one more way to be crushed, and anything that can relieve that pressure is a good thing, in my opinion.

Once you're older, you're better equipped to deal with the issue of personal appearance. You're more comfortable in your own skin, more confident, more secure. You're more likely to be satisfied with how you look, whether you're 'good-looking' or not. Of course not everyone reaches that level of maturity at the same age. Some people are there at sixteen, some don't get there until they're thirty or even older. But eighteen's the age of legal majority, when everyone's got the right to make their own decisions, and all you can do is trust your child and hope for the best.

Tamera Lyons:

It's been kind of an odd day for me. Good, but odd. I just got my calli turned off this morning.

Getting it turned off was easy. The nurse stuck some sensors on me and made me put on this helmet, and she showed me a bunch of pictures of people's faces.

Then she tapped at her keyboard for a minute, and said, 'I've switched off the calli,' just like that. I thought you might feel something when it happened, but you don't. Then she showed me the pictures again, to make sure it worked.

When I looked at the faces again, some of them seemed… different. Like they were glowing or more vivid or something. It's hard to describe. The nurse showed me my test results afterwards, and there were readings for how wide my pupils were dilating and how well my skin conducted electricity and stuff like that. And for the faces that seemed different, the readings went way up. She said those were the beautiful faces.

She said that I'd notice how other people's faces look right away, but it'd take a while before I had any reaction to how I looked. Supposedly you're too used to your face to tell.

And yeah, when I first looked in a mirror, I thought I looked totally the same. Since I got back from the doctor's, the people I see on campus definitely look different, but I still haven't noticed any difference in how I look. I've been looking at mirrors all day. For a while I was afraid that I was ugly and any minute the ugliness was going to appear, like a rash or something. And so I've been staring at the mirror, just waiting, and nothing's happened. So I figure I'm probably not really ugly or I'd have noticed it, but that means I'm not really pretty either, because I'd have noticed that too. So I guess that means I'm absolutely plain, you know? Exactly average. I guess that's okay.

TOLERANCE, RIGHTS AND RESPECT

DIVERSE SHORTS

May Malone, by David Almond

Connecting to the topic

This short story is about a boy's encounter with another boy, who has serious disabilities.

- Discuss in small groups what you know about how people with different disabilities are treated. You might consider their legal rights, the way they are treated by different people, the opportunities that are opened or closed to them, and so on.
- Share your thoughts with the whole class.

Connecting to the story

Although this story is called 'May Malone', in many ways it is more about the character of Norman.

- Rewrite the story, or a section of the story, in the voice of May. For example, you might write her thoughts about asking Norman to take her son, Alexander, outside.
- Share your stories around the class and discuss how you think your presentation of May compares to that of the writer, David Almond.

Connecting to the real world

Children with disabilities like Alexander in the story are no longer hidden away. They have a right to attend school and to have access to public places. This does not mean that all children have to be in the same class together, but it might mean that all children attend the same school, sometimes sharing lessons, sometimes not, depending on how appropriate this is.

- In a pair, or small group, come up with two lists and write down your ideas in a table as below:

1. Benefits for Alexander in attending a 'mainstream' school (with adaptations for his disabilities and needs as required).	2. Benefits for other children in being in a school with Alexander.

- Discuss your responses as a whole class. Consider whether or not you think a child like Alexander should be able to attend your school.

TOLERANCE, RIGHTS AND RESPECT

MAY MALONE

DAVID ALMOND

The story was that May Malone had a monster in her house. She kept it in chains. If you went round to the back of the house and put your ear to the wall you'd hear it groaning. You'd hear it howling at night, if you listened hard. There were stories about May and a priest from Blyth. There was a baby, it was said, but the baby was horrible because it was born from such a sin. Even weirder tales were whispered. The devil himself had come to May and it was the son of Satan, living in her house. She's been with horses, with dogs, with goats. Anyway, whatever it was you'd risk your body, your sanity and probably your soul if you got too close.

Norman Trench was ten or eleven at the time. He lived in the new flats in Felling Square. May's house was at the bottom end of Crimea Terrace, not far from the muddy green where the lads played football.

Norman's mam tightened her lips when he asked her about it.

'Them daft tales! Take no notice. What's done is done. Just keep away and leave her be.'

To look at May Malone, you'd never think she had a monster. She was getting on, but she wore tight skirts, she dyed her hair, and she wore high heels that clicked and clacked on the pavements as she hurried along. She was lapsed. Everyone knew the tale of how she'd stood up and cursed the priest in church itself, then stormed out, and never went again. You could see people's faces closing down as she hurried by. She rarely spoke to anybody and you could see that nobody wanted to speak to her. Except for some of the blokes who sighed, and followed her passing from the sides of their eyes.

Norman was a miserable kind of kid. Yes, he had some reasons – a brother that'd died, a dad that'd gone wrong with the drink. But everybody's got something to put up with. He just took everything too seriously. People used to go, 'Cheer up, lad. It might never bliddy happen.' And once or twice he yelled back. 'It's happened already, so bugger off!' He thought about death and dying all the time. He thought about the devil and Hell. He told the priest in confession about it once and the priest said, 'Ah, we all have great crosses to bear, my son.' He peered through the grille, trying to get a good look at Norman. 'Desolation of the heart can be a sign of God's call,' he said. 'Do you ever feel you might have a vocation, lad?'

His mam had been through everything he'd been through, of course, and worse. But she had a cheerful heart. 'Let's have a smile,' she'd say, and he'd curl his lips up and try to please her, but that just made things worse. 'Oh, son,' she'd say. 'Don't grow up so sad. God's good, the world is beautiful and heaven waits for us.' Made no difference. Norman believed in none of that. He was shutting down. He couldn't stop himself, even when the lads started moaning.

'Why can't you just enjoy yourself, man? You're like a wet bliddy Monday morning.'

And they started to turn their backs on him, like he was May Malone, or running away from him and howling, like he was her monster.

* * *

It was October when Norman went to May's for the first time. It was turning cold. The nights were cutting in. He waited till dark then he went down to the end of the terrace and into the back lane. He scrambled over the wall into her back yard. He went to the house wall and pressed his ear to it. Nothing. Maybe a radio somewhere far away. The distant voices of the lads echoing on the green. He concentrated. All he heard was his heart, then the noises of imaginary monsters inside himself. He tiptoed to the kitchen window and cupped his hands, peered in and nearly yelled with fright. But it was just his own staring eyes that goggled out at him. Nothing else.

* * *

Next time he went, though, he was sure there was a bit of grunting, a bit of squeaking. May came into the kitchen and made a pot of tea and put some biscuits on a plate. She looked out. Norman pressed right against the backyard wall. Then she leaned up and pulled the curtains shut. Norman climbed back out again and stood in the dark at the end of the terrace. He lit the cigarette he'd bought at Wiffen's shop that he'd said was for his mam. A river bell rang. A door clicked open and shut on Crimea Terrace and footsteps hurried up towards town. He drew deeply on the cigarette. He coughed. He stood looking down through the night towards the river. All this is getting me closer to hell, he thought.

'Where you been?' his mam said when he got back in.

'Football,' he said. 'With the lads.'

'Good. That might cheer you up, eh?'

TOLERANCE, RIGHTS AND RESPECT

He kept going back. Maybe he had it in his head that he'd be able to go to the lads and say, 'It's true. There is a monster. Come and see,' and that that'd sort everything out. But there was nothing, and soon the lads were taking no notice of him at all. It was like they didn't even see him, like he wasn't there. Probably they'd even forgotten all about the monster.

* * *

Then he stepped out of Wiffen's one afternoon and May Malone was right in front of him. She had a green coat on. Her eyes were green. Her fingernails were bright red.

'So,' she said. 'Would you like to see my monster?'

Norman gulped and blinked.

'Well?'

She didn't smile. She wasn't cross. Her voice was crisp and clear.

'Yes, please,' he said.

'You won't want to be seen walking with me. Follow me down in five minutes or so. Come to the front door.'

And she clacked away.

He smoked his fag as he walked down Crimea Terrace. He was trying to seem nonchalant.

The door was ajar.

'Don't just stand there,' she said from inside.

He sidled through. She was waiting in a narrow corridor. She put her hand across her mouth and widened her eyes.

'Oh no!' she said. 'You're inside May Malone's house! Lightning will strike at any moment!'

Everything was neat and clean, just like her. There was a door open to a living room. He saw a couple of armchairs, a couple of ashtrays. There was a decanter with what looked like whisky in it, and a couple of glasses. There was a painting of a Chinese lady on the hall wall. A red light was shining from upstairs.

She smiled. 'Come and see.'

She took him towards the back of the house.

'You won't tell anybody, of course,' she said. 'I decide who knows.'

She opened a door.

'This is my boy, Alexander.'

It was a small room. Light was coming in from a skylight in the ceiling. There was a narrow bed against the wall. A boy was sitting on a little blue sofa. His head was slumped onto his shoulder.

May knelt beside him and put her arm around him.

'Alexander,' she whispered. 'Here's a new visitor for you.'

She turned his head to Norman. One of his eyes wasn't there at all. The other was just a little crease in his face. The eye gleamed, like it was far away.

'His name is...' she whispered.

'Norman,' said Norman.

'Norman. Come closer, Norman.'

She looked at him.

'You're not going to hesitate *now*, are you?'

He knelt down beside them. She turned Alexander's head so that his eye was towards his visitor. She lifted his hand and rested it on Norman's face. Alexander grunted. He squeaked.

'Yes,' murmured May Malone. 'Yes, I know.'

She smiled.

'Alexander says you are very beautiful,' she said.

Norman couldn't help staring into the tiny distant eye.

'He says you are like an angel. And isn't *he* beautiful, too?' said May. '*Isn't* he?'

'Yes,' said Norman at last.

'Say hello. Go on. He can hear you, even though it might seem he can't.'

'Hello,' whispered Norman. 'Hello, Alexander.'

Alexander squeaked.

'See?' said May. 'He answers you. He is a boy, just like you. He is getting older, just like you are. He needs a friend. He needs to play.'

She sat on the edge of the bed. She smoothed her skirt over her knees and smiled at the two boys.

TOLERANCE, RIGHTS AND RESPECT

Alexander suddenly turned his face upwards. There was a pigeon on the skylight. His mouth pursed and he cooed.

'Yes!' said May. 'A bird and look at the clouds, Alexander.' He raised his hands and opened them over his head. 'See? He knows that the world is beautiful, Norman.'

Alexander trembled. Norman could feel the excitement rushing through the boy as the bird fluttered its wings above.

'Now,' said May. 'I would like you to take him out, Norman.'

Norman looked at the door and got ready to run. She smiled.

'Just into the yard at first,' she said. 'What could be difficult about that?'

Norman couldn't answer. Alexander's hand moved onto his and held it gently.

'Who's his father?' Norman dared to say.

'Ha! You *are* a nosey bugger, aren't you? Are you a churchgoer?'

'Yes.'

'I thought so. Those black-gowned priests. They blasted me. Don't let them blast you, Norman, with their 'Thou shalt nots.' She touched her boy's head. 'They said this angel is a devil. Never mind his father. Will you take him out?'

* * *

They helped Alexander from the sofa. May Malone opened the door. Norman held Alexander's arm and guided him out into the place where he'd only ever hidden in the dark. It was late afternoon. The sun was descending in the west. There were great streaks of red and gold across the sky. A storm of starlings swept over them from north to south. The city rumbled, the river bell rang, the lads' voices echoed from the green. Norman imagined walking towards them with May Malone's monster at his side. He imagined May Malone watching them all from a bench nearby. Alexander reached upward, upward and he moaned with joy. He held Norman and cooed into his ear. May Malone watched from the doorway.

'See? It's easy enough, isn't it?' she said.

They soon went back inside. They took Alexander to his room. He lay on the bed.

'Tired out,' said May.

She sat by him for a time.

'He is as he is because he is as he is. No other reason. And he is quite as capable of joy as any of us. More so, in fact.'

DIVERSE SHORTS

She leaned towards Norman.

'You, for instance,' she said, 'must stop being so sad. You know that, don't you?'

'Yes, Miss Malone.'

'Just open your eyes. The world is a strange and gorgeous and astonishing place.'

She looked at her watch.

'Now,' she said. 'You will come back again, won't you?'

'Yes, Miss Malone.'

'And you won't tell anybody, will you? Not until we're ready.'

'No, Miss Malone.'

'Good.'

She kissed his cheek. He said goodbye to Alexander. She led him to the door.

Norman walked up Crimea Terrace below the astonishing sky. He kept touching his cheek where May Malone's lipstick was, where the memory of her lips was. He kept remembering Alexander's tremble of excitement. A man was hurrying down, with the rim of his trilby tilted over his eyes.

'Hello,' said Norman.

The man flinched, looked at Norman in astonishment, then gave a broad grin.

'Aye, aye, lad' he said, and he winked.

Norman kept going. All the sadness was lifting away from him as he went uphill, like he was opening up, like everything was starting to be cleaned, like he was starting to see the world for the first time.

TOLERANCE, RIGHTS AND RESPECT

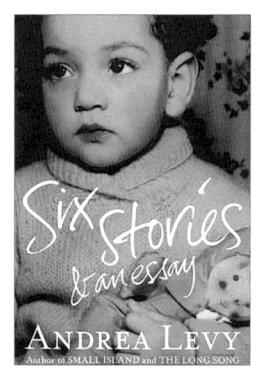

Loose Change, by Andrea Levy

- Read the whole of this story before attempting the 'Connecting to the topic' activity so that you do not spoil your reading experience.

Connecting to the topic

- Discuss as a whole class the different attitudes you have come across towards refugees?

How tolerant and respectful do you think people are towards refugees? What rights should they and do they have? What do you know about the British government's approach to refugees?

Connecting to the story

- Write down your thoughts and feelings about how the narrator behaves at the very end of this story. You might like to consider some of these questions.
    - What do you think about her decision at the end?
    - How might she have behaved differently, and what might have been the consequences?
    - Do you think most people would have behaved in the same way?
    - Would you have behaved differently?
    - Should her family history have influenced her behaviour?
    - How do you think her behaviour made Laylor feel?
- Share your responses round the class and use it to discuss what the writer is trying to make readers think and feel about the way we treat others.

Connecting to the real world

- In twos or threes discuss these statements about what you think the rights of refugees should be, identifying arguments for and against each one.
- Feed back to the class which statement your group agrees with most and why.

All refugees should be welcomed to Britain and encouraged to settle here.
All refugees should be welcomed to Britain and given help until their country is safe to return to.
Refugees should be given basic food and accommodation until they are able to return safely to their own country.

DIVERSE SHORTS

LOOSE CHANGE

ANDREA LEVY

I am not in the habit of making friends with strangers. I'm a Londoner. Not even little grey-haired old ladies passing comment on the weather can shame a response from me. I'm a Londoner – aloof sweats from my pores. But I was in a bit of a predicament; my period was two days early and I was caught unprepared.

I'd just gone into the National Portrait Gallery[1] to get out of the cold. It had begun to feel, as I'd walked through the bleak streets, like acid was being thrown at my exposed skin. My fingers were numb searching in my purse for change for the tampon machine; I barely felt the pull of the zip. But I didn't have any coins.

I was forced to ask in a loud voice in the small lavatory. 'Has anyone got three twenty-pence pieces?'

Everyone seemed to leave the place at once – all of them Londoners I was sure of it. Only she was left – fixing her hair in the mirror.

'Do you have change?'

She turned round slowly as I held out a ten pound note. She had the most spectacular eyebrows. I could see the lines of black hair, like magnetised iron filings, tumbling across her eyes and almost joining above her nose. I must have been staring hard to recall them so clearly now. She had wide black eyes and a round face with such a solid jawline that she looked to have taken a gentle whack from Tom and Jerry's cartoon frying pan. She dug into the pocket of her jacket and pulled out a bulging handful of money. It was coppers mostly. Some of it tinkled on to the floor. But she had change: too much – I didn't want a bag full of the stuff myself.

'Have you a five-pound note as well?' I asked.

She dropped the coins on to the basin area, spreading them out into the soapy puddles of water that were lying there. Then she said, 'You look?' She had an accent but I couldn't tell then where it was from; I thought maybe Spain.

---

1   Gallery in London displaying portraits – both good examples of the art and of famous people.

TOLERANCE, RIGHTS AND RESPECT

'Is this all you've got?' I asked. She nodded. 'Well look, let me just take this now …' I picked three coins out of the pile. 'Then I'll get some change in the shop and pay them back to you.' Her gaze was as keen as a cat with string. 'Do you understand – only I don't want all those coins?'

'Yes,' she said softly.

I was grateful. I took the money. But when I emerged from the cubicle, the girl and her handful of change were gone.

I found her again, staring at the portrait of Darcey Bussell[1]. She was inclining her head from one side to the other as if the painting were a dress she might soon try on for size.

I approached her about the money but she just said, 'This is good picture.'

Was it my explanation left dangling or the fact that she liked the dreadful painting that caused my mouth to gape?

'Really, you like it?' I said.

'She doesn't look real. It looks like…' Her eyelids fluttered sleepily as she searched for the right word. 'A dream.'

That particular picture always reminded me of the doodles girls drew in their rough books at school.

'You don't like?' she asked.

I shrugged.

'You show me one you like,' she said.

As I mentioned before I'm not in the habit of making friends with strangers, but there was something about this girl. Her eyes were encircled with dark shadows so that even when she smiled – introducing herself cheerfully as Laylor – they remained as mournful as a glum kid at a party. I took this fraternisation as defeat but I had to introduce her to a better portrait.

Alan Bennett[2] with his mysterious little brown bag didn't impress her at all. She preferred the photograph of David Beckham[3]. Germaine Greer[4] made her top lip curl and as for A.S. Byatt[5], she laughed out loud. 'This is child make this?'

---

1 Darcey Bussell is a well-known British ballet dancer.
2 Alan Bennett: British dramatist and essayist, well known for his dry humour.
3 David Beckham: England footballer and celebrity.
4 Germaine Greer: feminist academic.
5 A.S. Byatt: British novelist.

We were almost creating a scene. Laylor couldn't keep her voice down and people were beginning to watch us. I wanted to be released from my obligation.

'Look, let me buy us both a cup of tea,' I said. 'Then I can give you back your money.'

She brought out her handful of change again as we sat down at a table – eagerly passing it across for me to take some for the tea.

'No, I'll get this,' I said.

Her money jangled like a win on a slot machine as she tipped it back into her pocket. When I got back with the teas, I pushed over the twenty-pences I owed her. She began playing with them on the tabletop – pushing one around the other two in a figure of eight. Suddenly she leant towards me as if there were a conspiracy between us and said, 'I like art.' With that announcement a light briefly came on in those dull eyes to suggest that she was no more than eighteen. A student, perhaps.

'Where are you from?' I asked.

'Uzbekistan,' she said.

Was that the Balkans? I wasn't sure. 'Where is that?'

She licked her finger, then with great concentration drew an outline on to the tabletop. 'This is Uzbekistan,' she said. She licked her finger again to carefully plop a wet dot on to the map saying, 'And I come from here – Tashkent.'

'And where is all this?' I said, indicating the area around the little map with its slowly evaporating borders and town. She screwed up her face as if to say 'nowhere'.

'Are you on holiday?' I asked.

She nodded.

'How long are you here for?'

Leaning her elbows on the table she took a sip of her tea. 'Ehh, it is bitter!' she shouted.

'Put some sugar in it,' I said, pushing the sugar sachets toward her.

She was reluctant. 'Is for free?' she asked.

'Yes, take one.'

The sugar spilled as she clumsily opened the packet. I laughed it off but she, with the focus of a prayer, put her cup up to the edge of the table and swept the sugar into it with the side of her hand. The rest of the detritus that was on the tabletop fell into the tea as well. Some crumbs, a tiny scrap of paper and a curly black hair floated on the surface of the drink. I felt sick as she put the cup back to her mouth.

TOLERANCE, RIGHTS AND RESPECT

'Pour that one away, I'll get you another one.'

Just as I said that a young boy arrived at our table and stood legs astride before her. He pushed down the hood on his padded coat. His head was curious – flat as a cardboard cut-out – with hair stuck to his sweaty forehead in black curlicues. And his face was as doggedly determined as two fists raised. They began talking in whatever language it was they spoke. Laylor's tone was pleading; the boy's aggrieved. Laylor took the money from her pocket and held it up to him. She slapped his hand away when he tried to wrest all the coins from her palm. Then, as abruptly as he had appeared, he left. Laylor called something after him. Everyone turned to stare at her, except the boy who just carried on

'Who was that?'

With the teacup resting on her lip, she said, 'my brother. He wants to know where we sleep tonight.'

'Oh yes, where's that?' I was rummaging through the contents of my bag for a tissue, so it was casually asked.

'It's square we have slept before.'

'Which hotel is it?' I thought of the Russell Hotel, that was on a square – uniformed attendants, bed-turning-down facilities, old-world style.

She was picking the curly black hair off her tongue when she said, 'No hotel, just the square.'

It was then that I began to notice things I had not seen before… dirt under each of her chipped fingernails, the collar of her blouse crumpled and unironed, a tiny cut on her cheek, a fringe that looked to have been cut with blunt nail clippers. I found a tissue and used it to wipe my sweating palms.

'How do you mean, just the square?'

'We sleep out in the square,' she said. She spread her hands to suggest the lie of her bed.

'Outside?'

She nodded.

'Tonight?'

'Yes.'

The memory of the bitter cold still tingled at my fingertips as I said, 'Why?'

It took her no more than two breaths to tell me the story. She and her brother had had to leave their country, Uzbekistan, when their parents – who were

journalists – were arrested. It was arranged very quickly – friends of their parents acquired passports for them and put them on to a plane. They had been in England for three days but they knew no one here. This country was just a safe place. Now all the money they had could be lifted in the palm of a hand to a stranger in a toilet. So they were sleeping rough – in the shelter of a square, covered in blankets, on top of some cardboard.

At the next table a woman was complaining loudly that there was too much froth on her coffee. Her companion was relating the miserable tale of her daughter's attempt to get into publishing. What did they think about the strange girl sitting opposite me? Nothing. Only I knew what a menacing place Laylor's world had become.

She'd lost a tooth. I noticed the ugly gap when she smiled at me saying, 'I love London.'

She had sought me out – sifted me from the crowd. This young woman was desperate for help. She'd even cunningly made me obliged to her.

'I have a picture of Tower Bridge at home on wall although I have not seen yet.'

But why me? I had my son to think of. Why pick on a single mother with a nine-year old? We haven't got the time. Those two women at the next table, with their matching handbags and shoes, they did nothing but lunch. Why hadn't she approached them instead?

'From little girl, I always want to see it…' she went on.

I didn't know anything about people in her situation. Didn't they have to go somewhere? Croydon, was it? Couldn't she have gone to the police? Or some charity? My life was hard enough without this stranger tramping through it. She smelt of mildewed washing. Imagine her dragging that awful stink into my kitchen. Cupping her filthy hands round my bone china. Smearing my white linen. Her big face with its pantomime eyebrows leering over my son. Slumping on to my sofa and kicking off her muddy boots as she yanked me down into her particular hell. How would I ever get rid of her?

'You know where is Tower Bridge?'

Perhaps there was something tender-hearted in my face.

When my grandma first came to England from the Caribbean she lived through days as lonely and cold as an open grave. The story she told her grandchildren was about the stranger who woke her while she was sleeping in a doorway and offered her a warm bed for the night. It was this act of benevolence that kept my grandmother alive. She was convinced of it. Her Good Samaritan.

TOLERANCE, RIGHTS AND RESPECT

'Is something wrong?' the girl asked.

Now my grandmother talks with passion about scrounging refugees[1]; those asylum seekers who can't even speak the language, storming the country and making it difficult for her and everyone else.

'Last week …' she began, her voice quivering, 'I was in home.'

This was embarrassing. I couldn't turn the other way, the girl was staring straight at me.

'This day, Friday,' she went on, 'I cooked fish for my mother and brother.'

The whites of her eyes were becoming soft and pink; she was going to cry.

'This day Friday I am here in London,' she said. 'And I worry I will not see my mother again.'

Only a savage would turn away when it was merely kindness that was needed.

I resolved to help her. I had warm bedrooms, one of them empty. I would make her dinner. Fried chicken or maybe poached fish in wine. I would run her a bath filled with bubbles. Wrap her in thick towels heated on a rail. I would hunt out some warm clothes and after I had put my son to bed I would make her cocoa. We would sit and talk. I would let her tell me all that she had been through. Wipe her tears and assure her that she was now safe. I would phone a colleague from school and ask him for advice. Then in the morning I would take Laylor to wherever she needed to go. And before we said goodbye I would press my phone number into her hand.

All Laylor's grandchildren would know my name.

Her nose was running with snot. She pulled down the sleeve of her jacket to drag it across her face and said, 'I must find my brother.'

I didn't have any more tissues. 'I'll get you something to wipe your nose,' I said. I got up from the table.

She watched me, frowning; the tiny hairs of her eyebrows locking together like Velcro.

I walked to the counter where serviettes were lying in a neat pile. I picked up four. Then standing straight I walked on. Not back to Laylor but up the stairs to the exit.

I pushed through the revolving doors and threw myself into the cold.

---

[1] A refugee is a person who has been forced to leave their country in order to escape war, persecution, or natural disaster

DIVERSE SHORTS

Brownies, by ZZ Packer

Connecting to the topic

This short story centres around the girls from a Brownie troop in America. The girls are all black and make fun of girls from other troops because they are white.

People are discriminated against for many different reasons. For example, it might be to do with the colour of their skin, or their sexuality, or because they have a disability.

- As a class, discuss why people might discriminate against others. What, for example, might it say about their own values, sense of belonging, or upbringing?
- Discuss whether it is any more or less acceptable for people to discriminate against others because they themselves belong to a minority group. For example, is there a difference between black children making fun of white children, compared to white children making fun of black children? What kind of story would you expect depending on which way round this was?

Connecting to the story

- Imagine you are one of the characters from the narrator's Brownie troop looking back years later, as an adult, on the events described in the story.
- In character, write down your thoughts, focusing on:
    - What you think about the way that you and the other girls in your troop behaved, and why you all behaved in this way.
    - Your thoughts about why different 'minority' groups were sent to the same camp – so black girls were sent to the same camp as white girls with learning difficulties.
- Share your writing round the class.

Connecting to real life

- In a small group, develop an argument around the statement below. You can either support it or oppose it.

> Different minority groups have a responsibility to support each other.

- Either hold a small debate in your class around the statement, or each write down your own thoughts and read out a selection round the class.

TOLERANCE, RIGHTS AND RESPECT

BROWNIES

ZZ PACKER

By our second day at Camp Crescendo, the girls in my Brownie troop had decided to kick the asses of each and every girl in Brownie Troop 909. Troop 909 was doomed from the first day of camp; they were white girls, their complexions a blend of ice cream: strawberry, vanilla. They turtled out from their bus in pairs, their rolled-up sleeping bags chromatised with Disney characters: Sleeping Beauty, Snow White, Mickey Mouse; or the generic ones cheap parents bought: washed-out rainbows, unicorns, curly-eyelashed frogs. Some clutched Igloo coolers and still others held on to stuffed toys like pacifiers, looking all around them like tourists determined to be dazzled.

Our troop was wending its way past their bus, past the ranger station, past the colourful trail guide drawn like a treasure map, locked behind glass.

'Man, did you smell them?' Arnetta said, giving the girls a slow once-over, 'They smell like Chihuahuas. *Wet* Chihuahuas.' Their troop was still at the entrance, and though we had passed them by yards, Arnetta raised her nose in the air and grimaced.

Arnetta said this from the very rear of the line, far away from Mrs. Margolin, who always strung our troop behind her like a brood of obedient ducklings. Mrs. Margolin even looked like a mother duck – she had hair cropped close to a small ball of a head, almost no neck, and huge, miraculous breasts. She wore enormous belts that looked like the kind that weightlifters wear, except hers would be cheap metallic gold or rabbit fur or covered with gigantic fake sunflowers, and often these belts would become nature lessons in and of themselves. 'See,' Mrs. Margolin once said to us, pointing to her belt, 'this one's made entirely from the feathers of baby pigeons.'

The belt layered with feathers was uncanny enough, but I was more disturbed by the realisation that I had never actually *seen* a baby pigeon. I searched weeks for one, in vain – scampering after pigeons whenever I was downtown with my father.

But nature lessons were not Mrs. Margolin's top priority. She saw the position of troop leader as an evangelical post. Back at the A.M.E. church where our Brownie meetings were held, Mrs. Margolin was especially fond of imparting religious aphorisms by means of acrostics – 'Satan' was the 'Serpent Always Tempting and

DIVERSE SHORTS

Noisesome'; she'd refer to the 'Bible' as 'Basic Instructions Before Leaving Earth.' Whenever she quizzed us on these, expecting to hear the acrostics parroted back to her, only Arnetta's correct replies soared over our vague mumblings. 'Jesus?' Mrs. Margolin might ask expectantly, and Arnetta alone would dutifully answer, 'Jehovah's Example, Saving Us Sinners.'

Arnetta always made a point of listening to Mrs. Margolin's religious talk and giving her what she wanted to hear. Because of this, Arnetta could have blared through a megaphone that the white girls of Troop 909 were 'wet Chihuahuas' without so much as a blink from Mrs. Margolin. Once, Arnetta killed the troop goldfish by feeding it a french fry covered in ketchup, and when Mrs. Margolin demanded that she explain what had happened, claimed the goldfish had been eyeing her meal for *hours*, then the fish – giving in to temptation – had leapt up and snatched a whole golden fry from her fingertips.

'*Serious* Chihuahua,' Octavia added, and though neither Arnetta nor Octavia could *spell* 'Chihuahua,' had never *seen* a Chihuahua, trisyllabic words had gained a sort of exoticism within our fourth grade set at Woodrow Wilson Elementary. Arnetta and Octavia would flip through the dictionary, determined to work the vulgar sounding ones like 'Djibouti' and 'asinine' into conversation.

'*Caucasian* Chihuahuas,' Arnetta said.

That did it. The girls in my troop turned elastic: Drema and Elise doubled up on one another like inextricably entwined kites; Octavia slapped her belly; Janice jumped straight up in the air, then did it again, as if to slam-dunk her own head. They could not stop laughing. No one had laughed so hard since a boy named Martez had stuck a pencil in the electric socket and spent the whole day with a strange grin on his face.

'Girls, girls,' said our parent helper, Mrs. Hedy. Mrs. Hedy was Octavia's mother, and she wagged her index finger perfunctorily, like a windshield wiper. 'Stop it, now. Be good.' She said this loud enough to be heard, but lazily, bereft of any feeling or indication that she meant to be obeyed, as though she could say these words again at the exact same pitch if a button somewhere on her were pressed.

But the rest of the girls didn't stop; they only laughed louder. It was the word 'Caucasian' that got them all going. One day at school, about a month before the Brownie camping trip, Arnetta turned to a boy wearing impossibly high-ankled floodwater jeans and said, 'What are you? *Caucasian*?' The word took off from there, and soon everything was Caucasian. If you ate too fast you ate like a Caucasian, if you ate too slow you ate like a Caucasian. The biggest feat anyone at Woodrow Wilson could do was to jump off the swing in midair, at the highest point in its arc, and if you fell (as I had, more than once) instead of landing on your

TOLERANCE, RIGHTS AND RESPECT

feet, knees bent Olympic gymnast-style, Arnetta and Octavia were prepared to comment. They'd look at each other with the silence of passengers who'd narrowly escaped an accident, then nod their heads, whispering with solemn horror, *'Caucasian.'*

Even the only white kid in our school, Dennis, got in on the Caucasian act. That time when Martez stuck a pencil in the socket, Dennis had pointed and yelled, 'That was *so* Caucasian!'

* * *

When you lived in the south suburbs of Atlanta, it was easy to forget about whites. Whites were like those baby pigeons: real and existing, but rarely seen or thought about. Everyone had been to Rich's to go clothes shopping, everyone had seen white girls and their mothers coo-cooing over dresses; everyone had gone to the downtown library and seen white businessmen swish by importantly, wrists flexed in front of them to check the time as though they would change from Clark Kent into Superman at any second. But those images were as fleeting as cards shuffled in a deck, whereas the ten white girls behind us – *invaders*, Arnetta would later call them – were instantly real and memorable, with their long, shampoo-commercial hair, straight as spaghetti from the box. This alone was reason for envy and hatred. The only black girl most of us had ever seen with hair that long was Octavia, whose hair hung past her butt like a Hawaiian hula dancer's. The sight of Octavia's mane prompted other girls to listen to her reverentially, as though whatever she had to say would somehow activate their own follicles. For example, when, on the first day of camp, Octavia made as if to speak, and everyone fell silent. 'Nobody,' Octavia said, 'calls us niggers.'

At the end of that first day, when half of our troop made their way back to the cabin after tag-team restroom visits, Arnetta said she'd heard one of the Troop 909 girls call Daphne a nigger. The other half of the girls and I were helping Mrs. Margolin clean up the pots and pans from the campfire ravioli dinner. When we made our way to the restrooms to wash up and brush our teeth, we met up with Arnetta midway.

'Man, I completely heard the girl,' Arnetta reported. 'Right, Daphne?'

Daphne hardly ever spoke, but when she did, her voice was petite and tinkly, the voice one might expect from a shiny new earring. She'd written a poem once, for Langston Hughes Day, a poem brimming with all the teacher-winning ingredients – trees and oceans, sunsets and moons – but what cinched the poem for the grown-ups, snatching the win from Octavia's musical ode to Grandmaster Flash and the Furious Five, were Daphne's last lines:

DIVERSE SHORTS

You are my father, the veteran
When you cry in the dark
It rains and rains and rains in my heart

She'd always worn clean, though faded, jumpers and dresses when Chic jeans were the fashion, but when she went up to the dais to receive her prize journal, pages trimmed in gold, she wore a new dress with a velveteen bodice and a taffeta skirt as wide as an umbrella. All the kids clapped, though none of them understood the poem. I'd read encyclopaedias the way others read comics, and I didn't get it. But those last lines pricked me, they were so eerie, and as my father and I ate cereal, I'd whisper over my Froot Loops, like a mantra, *'You are my father, the veteran. You are my father, the veteran, the veteran, the veteran,'* until my father, who acted in plays as Caliban and Othello and was not a veteran, marched me up to my teacher one morning and said, 'Can you tell me what's wrong with this kid?'

I thought Daphne and I might become friends, but I think she grew spooked by me whispering those lines to her, begging her to tell me what they meant, and I soon understood that two quiet people like us were better off quiet alone.

'Daphne? Didn't you hear them call you a nigger?' Arnetta asked, giving Daphne a nudge.

The sun was setting behind the trees, and their leafy tops formed a canopy of black lace for the flame of the sun to pass through. Daphne shrugged her shoulders at first, then slowly nodded her head when Arnetta gave her a hard look.

Twenty minutes later, when my restroom group returned to the cabin, Arnetta was still talking about Troop 909. My restroom group had passed by some of the 909 girls. For the most part, they deferred to us, waving us into the restrooms, letting us go even though they'd gotten there first.

We'd seen them, but from afar, never within their orbit enough to see whether their faces were the way all white girls appeared on TV – ponytailed and full of energy, bubbling over with love and money. All I could see was that some of them rapidly fanned their faces with their hands, though the heat of the day had long passed. A few seemed to be lolling their heads in slow circles, half purposefully, as if exercising the muscles of their necks, half ecstatically, like Stevie Wonder.

'We can't let them get away with that,' Arnetta said, dropping her voice to a laryngitic whisper. 'We can't let them get away with calling us niggers. I say we teach them a lesson.' She sat down cross-legged on a sleeping bag, an embittered Buddha, eyes glimmering acrylic-black. 'We can't go telling Mrs. Margolin, either. Mrs. Margolin'll say something about doing unto others and the path of righteousness and all. Forget that shit.' She let her eyes flutter irreverently till they half closed, as though ignoring an insult not worth returning. We could all hear Mrs. Margolin outside, gathering the last of the metal campware.

TOLERANCE, RIGHTS AND RESPECT

Nobody said anything for a while. Usually people were quiet after Arnetta spoke. Her tone had an upholstered confidence that was somehow both regal and vulgar at once. It demanded a few moments of silence in its wake, like the ringing of a church bell or the playing of taps. Sometimes Octavia would ditto or dissent to whatever Arnetta had said, and this was the signal that others could speak. But this time Octavia just swirled a long cord of hair into pretzel shapes.

'Well?' Arnetta said. She looked as if she had discerned the hidden severity of the situation and was waiting for the rest of us to catch up. Everyone looked from Arnetta to Daphne. It was, after all, Daphne who had supposedly been called the name, but Daphne sat on the bare cabin floor, flipping through the pages of the Girl Scout handbook, eyebrows arched in mock wonder, as if the handbook were a catalogue full of bright and startling foreign costumes. Janice broke the silence. She clapped her hands to broach her idea of a plan. 'They gone be sleeping,' she whispered conspiratorially, 'then we gone sneak into they cabin, then we'll put daddy longlegs in they sleeping bags. Then they'll wake up. Then we gone beat 'em up till they're as flat as frying pans!' She jammed her fist into the palm of her hand, then made a sizzling sound.

Janice's country accent was laughable, her looks homely, her jumpy acrobatics embarrassing to behold. Arnetta and Octavia volleyed amused, arrogant smiles whenever Janice opened her mouth, but Janice never caught the hint, spoke whenever she wanted, fluttered around Arnetta and Octavia futilely offering her opinions to their departing backs. Whenever Arnetta and Octavia shooed her away, Janice loitered until the two would finally sigh and ask, 'What *is* it, Miss Caucausoid? What do you *want*?'

'Shut up, Janice,' Octavia said, letting a fingered loop of hair fall to her waist as though just the sound of Janice's voice had ruined the fun of her hair twisting.

Janice obeyed, her mouth hung open in a loose grin, unflappable, unhurt.

'All right,' Arnetta said, standing up. 'We're going to have a secret meeting and talk about what we're going to do.'

Everyone gravely nodded her head. The word 'secret' had a built-in importance, the modifier form of the word carried more clout than the noun. A secret meant nothing; it was like gossip: just a bit of unpleasant knowledge about someone who happened to be someone other than yourself. A secret *meeting*, or a secret *club* was entirely different.

That was when Arnetta turned to me as though she knew that doing so was both a compliment and a charity.

'Snot, you're not going to be a bitch and tell Mrs. Margolin, are you?'

I had been called 'Snot' ever since first grade, when I'd sneezed in class and two long ropes of mucus had splattered a nearby girl.

'Hey,' I said. "Maybe you didn't hear them right – I mean –'

'Are you gonna tell on us or not?' was all Arnetta wanted to know, and by the time the question was asked, the rest of our Brownie troop looked at me as though they'd already decided their course of action, me being the only impediment.

* * *

Camp Crescendo used to double as a high-school-band and field hockey camp until an arcing field hockey ball landed on the clasp of a girl's metal barrette, knifing a skull nerve and paralysing the right side of her body. The camp closed down for a few years and the girl's teammates built a memorial, filling the spot on which the girl fell with hockey balls, on which they had painted – all in nail polish – get-well tidings, flowers, and hearts. The balls were still stacked there, like a shrine of ostrich eggs embedded in the ground.

On the second day of camp, Troop 909 was dancing around the mound of hockey balls, their limbs jangling awkwardly, their cries like the constant summer squeal of an amusement park. There was a stream that bordered the field hockey lawn, and the girls from my troop settled next to it, scarfing down the last of lunch: sandwiches made from salami and slices of tomato that had gotten waterlogged from the melting ice in the cooler. From the stream bank, Arnetta eyed the Troop 909 girls, scrutinising their movements to glean inspiration for battle.

'Man,' Arnetta said, 'we could bumrush them right now if that damn lady would *leave*.'

The 909 troop leader was a white woman with the severe pageboy hairdo of an ancient Egyptian. She lay on a picnic blanket, sphinx-like, eating a banana, sometimes holding it out in front of her like a microphone. Beside her sat a girl slowly flapping one hand like a bird with a broken wing. Occasionally, the leader would call out the names of girls who'd attempted leapfrogs and flips, or of girls who yelled too loudly or strayed far from the circle.

'I'm just glad Big Fat Mama's not following us here,' Octavia said. 'At least we don't have to worry about her.' Mrs. Margolin, Octavia assured us, was having her Afternoon Devotional, shrouded in mosquito netting, in a clearing she'd found. Mrs. Hedy was cleaning mud from her espadrilles in the cabin.

'I handled them.' Arnetta sucked on her teeth and proudly grinned. 'I told her we was going to gather leaves.'

'Gather leaves,' Octavia said, nodding respectfully. 'That's a good one. Especially since they're so mad-crazy about this camping thing.' She looked from ground

TOLERANCE, RIGHTS AND RESPECT

to sky, sky to ground. Her hair hung down her back in two braids like a squaw's. 'I mean, I really don't know why it's even called *camping* – all we ever do with Nature is find some twigs and say something like, 'Wow, this fell from a tree."' She then studied her sandwich. With two disdainful fingers, she picked out a slice of dripping tomato, the sections congealed with red slime. She pitched it into the stream embrowned with dead leaves and the murky effigies of other dead things, but in the opaque water, a group of small silver-brown fish appeared. They surrounded the tomato and nibbled.

'Look!' Janice cried. 'Fishes! Fishes!' As she scrambled to the edge of the stream to watch, a covey of insects threw up tantrums from the wheatgrass and nettle, a throng of tiny electric machines, all going at once. Octavia sneaked up behind Janice as if to push her in. Daphne and I exchanged terrified looks. It seemed as though only we knew that Octavia was close enough – and bold enough – to actually push Janice into the stream. Janice turned around quickly, but Octavia was already staring serenely into the still water as though she was gathering some sort of courage from it. 'What's so funny?' Janice said, eyeing them all suspiciously.

Elise began humming the tune to 'Karma Chameleon', all the girls joining in, their hums light and facile. Janice also began to hum, against everyone else, the high-octane opening chords of 'Beat It.'

'I love me some Michael Jackson,' Janice said when she'd finished humming, smacking her lips as though Michael Jackson were a favourite meal. 'I *will* marry Michael Jackson.'

Before anyone had a chance to impress upon Janice the impossibility of this, Arnetta suddenly rose, made a sun visor of her hand, and watched Troop 909 leave the field hockey lawn.

'Dammit!' she said. 'We've got to get them *alone*.'

'They won't ever be alone,' I said. All the rest of the girls looked at me, for I usually kept quiet. If I spoke even a word, I could count on someone calling me Snot. Everyone seemed to think that we could beat up these girls; no one entertained the thought that they might fight *back*. 'The only time they'll be unsupervised is in the bathroom.'

'Oh shut up, Snot,' Octavia said.

But Arnetta slowly nodded her head. 'The bathroom,' she said. 'The bathroom,' she said, again and again. 'The bathroom! The bathroom!

* * *

According to Octavia's watch, it took us five minutes to hike to the restrooms, which were midway between our cabin and Troop 909's. Inside, the mirrors above the sinks returned only the vaguest of reflections, as though someone had taken a scouring pad to their surfaces to obscure the shine. Pine needles, leaves, and dirty, flattened wads of chewing gum covered the floor like a mosaic. Webs of hair matted the drain in the middle of the floor. Above the sinks and below the mirrors, stacks of folded white paper towels lay on a long metal counter. Shaggy white balls of paper towels sat on the sinktops in a line like corsages on display. A thread of floss snaked from a wad of tissues dotted with the faint red-pink of blood. One of those white girls, I thought, had just lost a tooth.

Though the restroom looked almost the same as it had the night before, it somehow seemed stranger now. We hadn't noticed the wooden rafters coming together in great V's. We were, it seemed, inside a whale, viewing the ribs of the roof of its mouth.

'Wow. It's a mess,' Elise said.

'You can say that again.'

Arnetta leaned against the doorjamb of a restroom stall. 'This is where they'll be again,' she said. Just seeing the place, just having a plan seemed to satisfy her. 'We'll go in and talk to them. You know, 'How you doing? How long'll you be here?' That sort of thing. Then Octavia and I are gonna tell them what happens when they call any one of us a nigger.'

'I'm going to say something too,' Janice said.

Arnetta considered this. 'Sure,' she said. 'Of course. Whatever you want.'

Janice pointed her finger like a gun at Octavia and rehearsed the line she'd thought up, "We're gonna teach you a *lesson*!' That's what I'm going to say.' She narrowed her eyes like a TV mobster. "We're gonna teach you little girls a lesson!"

With the back of her hand, Octavia brushed Janice's finger away. 'You couldn't teach me to shit in a toilet.'

'But,' I said, 'what if they say, 'We didn't say that? We didn't call anyone an N-I-G-G-E-R."

'Snot,' Arnetta said, and then sighed. 'Don't think. Just fight. If you even know how.'

Everyone laughed except Daphne. Arnetta gently laid her hand on Daphne's shoulder. 'Daphne. You don't have to fight. We're doing this for you.'

Daphne walked to the counter, took a clean paper towel, and carefully unfolded it like a map. With it, she began to pick up the trash all around. Everyone watched.

TOLERANCE, RIGHTS AND RESPECT

'C'mon,' Arnetta said to everyone. 'Let's beat it.' We all ambled toward the doorway, where the sunshine made one large white rectangle of light. We were immediately blinded, and we shielded our hands and our forearms.

'Daphne?' Arnetta asked. 'Are you coming?'

We all looked back at the bending girl, the thin of her back hunched like the back of a custodian sweeping a stage, caught in limelight. Stray strands of her hair were lit near-transparent, thin fibre-optic threads. She did not nod yes to the question, nor did she shake her head no. She abided, bent. Then she began again, picking up leaves, wads of paper, the cotton fluff innards from a torn stuffed toy. She did it so methodically, so exquisitely, so humbly, she must have been trained. I thought of those dresses she wore, faded and old, yet so pressed and clean. I then saw the poverty in them; I then could imagine her mother, cleaning the houses of others, returning home, weary.

'I guess she's not coming.'

We left her and headed back to our cabin, over pine needles and leaves, taking the path full of shade.

'What about our secret meeting?' Elise asked.

Arnetta enunciated her words in a way that defied contradiction: 'We just had it.'

* * *

It was nearing our bedtime, but the sun had not yet set.

'Hey, your mama's coming,' Arnetta said to Octavia when she saw Mrs. Hedy walk toward the cabin, sniffling. When Octavia's mother wasn't giving bored, parochial orders, she sniffled continuously, mourning an imminent divorce from her husband. She might begin a sentence, 'I don't know what Robert will do when Octavia and I are gone. Who'll buy him cigarettes?' and Octavia would hotly whisper, '*Mama*,' in a way that meant: Please don't talk about our problems in front of everyone. Please shut up.

But when Mrs. Hedy began talking about her husband, thinking about her husband, seeing clouds shaped like the head of her husband, she couldn't be quiet, and no one could dislodge her from the comfort of her own woe. Only one thing could perk her up – Brownie songs. If the girls were quiet, and Mrs. Hedy was in her dopey, sorrowful mood, she would say, 'Y'all know I like those songs, girls. Why don't you sing one?' Everyone would groan, except me and Daphne. I, for one, liked some of the songs.

'C'mon, everybody,' Octavia said drearily. 'She likes the Brownie song best.'

We sang, loud enough to reach Mrs. Hedy:

'I've got something in my pocket;
It belongs across my face.
And I keep it very close at hand in a most convenient place.
I'm sure you couldn't guess it
If you guessed a long, long while.
So I'll take it out and put it on –
It's a great big Brownie smile!'

The Brownie song was supposed to be sung cheerfully, as though we were elves in a workshop, singing as we merrily cobbled shoes, but everyone except me hated the song so much that they sang it like a maudlin record, played on the most sluggish of rpms.

'That was good,' Mrs. Hedy said, closing the cabin door behind her. 'Wasn't that nice, Linda?'

'Praise God,' Mrs. Margolin answered without raising her head from the chore of counting out Popsicle sticks for the next day's craft session.

'Sing another one,' Mrs. Hedy said. She said it with a sort of joyful aggression, like a drunk I'd once seen who'd refused to leave a Korean grocery.

'God, Mama, get over it,' Octavia whispered in a voice meant only for Arnetta, but Mrs. Hedy heard it and started to leave the cabin.

'Don't go,' Arnetta said. She ran after Mrs. Hedy and held her by the arm. 'We haven't finished singing.' She nudged us with a single look. 'Let's sing the 'Friends Song.' For Mrs. Hedy.'

Although I liked some of the songs, I hated this one:

Make new friends
But keep the o-old,
One is silver
And the other gold.

If most of the girls in the troop could be any type of metal, they'd be bunched-up wads of tinfoil, maybe, or rusty iron nails you had to get tetanus shots for.

'No, no, no,' Mrs. Margolin said before anyone could start in on the 'Friends Song.' 'An uplifting song. Something to lift her up and take her mind off all these earthly burdens.'

Arnetta and Octavia rolled their eyes. Everyone knew what song Mrs. Margolin was talking about, and no one, no one, wanted to sing it.

'Please, no,' a voice called out. 'Not 'The Doughnut Song."

'Please not 'The Doughnut Song," Octavia pleaded.

'I'll brush my teeth two times if I don't have to sing 'The Doughnut –"

TOLERANCE, RIGHTS AND RESPECT

'Sing!' Mrs. Margolin demanded. We sang:

'Life without Jesus is like a do-ough-nut!
Like a do-ooough-nut!
Like a do-ooough-nut!
Life without Jesus is like a do-ough-nut!
There's a hole in the middle of my soul!'

There were other verses, involving other pastries, but we stopped after the first one and cast glances toward Mrs. Margolin to see if we could gain a reprieve. Mrs. Margolin's eyes fluttered blissfully. She was half asleep.

'Awww,' Mrs. Hedy said, as though giant Mrs. Margolin were a cute baby, 'Mrs. Margolin's had a long day.'

'Yes indeed,' Mrs. Margolin answered. 'If you don't mind, I might just go to the lodge where the beds are. I haven't been the same since the operation.'

I had not heard of this operation, or when it had occurred, since Mrs. Margolin had never missed the once-a-week Brownie meetings, but I could see from Daphne's face that she was concerned, and I could see that the other girls had decided that Mrs. Margolin's operation must have happened long ago in some remote time unconnected to our own. Nevertheless, they put on sad faces. We had all been taught that adulthood was full of sorrow and pain, taxes and bills, dreaded work and dealings with whites, sickness and death. I tried to do what the others did. I tried to look silent.

'Go right ahead, Linda,' Mrs. Hedy said. 'I'll watch the girls.' Mrs. Hedy seemed to forget about divorce for a moment; she looked at us with dewy eyes, as if we were mysterious, furry creatures. Meanwhile, Mrs. Margolin walked through the maze of sleeping bags until she found her own. She gathered a neat stack of clothes and pyjamas slowly, as though doing so was almost painful. She took her toothbrush, her toothpaste, her pillow. 'All right!' Mrs. Margolin said, addressing us all from the threshold of the cabin. 'Be in bed by nine.' She said it with a twinkle in her voice, letting us know she was allowing us to be naughty and stay up till nine-fifteen.

'C'mon everybody,' Arnetta said after Mrs. Margolin left. 'Time for us to wash up.'

Everyone watched Mrs. Hedy closely, wondering whether she would insist on coming with us since it was night, making a fight with Troop 909 nearly impossible. Troop 909 would soon be in the bathroom, washing their faces, brushing their teeth – completely unsuspecting of our ambush.

'We won't be long,' Arnetta said. 'We're old enough to go to the restrooms by ourselves.'

Ms. Hedy pursed her lips at this dilemma. 'Well, I guess you Brownies are almost Girl Scouts, right?'

'Right!'

'Just one more badge,' Drema said.

'And about,' Octavia droned, 'a million more cookies to sell.' Octavia looked at all of us. *Now's our chance*, her face seemed to say, but our chance to do what, I didn't exactly know.

Finally, Mrs. Hedy walked to the doorway where Octavia stood dutifully waiting to say goodbye but looking bored doing it. Mrs. Hedy held Octavia's chin. 'You'll be good?'

'Yes, Mama.'

'And remember to pray for me and your father? If I'm asleep when you get back?'

'Yes, Mama.'

* * *

When the other girls had finished getting their toothbrushes and washcloths and flashlights for the group restroom trip, I was drawing pictures of tiny birds with too many feathers. Daphne was sitting on her sleeping bag, reading.

'You're not going to come?' Octavia asked. Daphne shook her head.

'I'm gonna stay, too,' I said. 'I'll go to the restroom when Daphne and Mrs. Hedy go.'

Arnetta leaned down toward me and whispered so that Mrs. Hedy, who'd taken over Mrs. Margolin's task of counting Popsicle sticks, couldn't hear. 'No, Snot. If we get in trouble, you're going to get in trouble with the rest of us.'

* * *

We made our way through the darkness by flashlight. The tree branches that had shaded us just hours earlier, along the same path, now looked like arms sprouting menacing hands. The stars sprinkled the sky like spilled salt. They seemed fastened to the darkness, high up and holy, their places fixed and definite as we stirred beneath them.

Some, like me, were quiet because we were afraid of the dark; others were talking like crazy for the same reason.

'Wow!' Drema said, looking up. 'Why are all the stars out here? I never see stars back on Oneida Street.'

'It's a camping trip, that's why,' Octavia said. 'You're supposed to see stars on camping trips.'

TOLERANCE, RIGHTS AND RESPECT

Janice said, 'This place smells like my mother's air freshener.'

'These woods are *pine*,' Elise said. 'Your mother probably uses *pine* air freshener.'

Janice mouthed an exaggerated 'Oh,' nodding her head as though she just then understood one of the world's great secrets.

No one talked about fighting. Everyone was afraid enough just walking through the infinite deep of the woods. Even though I didn't like to fight, was afraid of fighting, I felt I was part of the rest of the troop; like I was defending something. We trudged against the slight incline of the path, Arnetta leading the way.

'You know,' I said, 'their leader will be there. Or they won't even be there. It's dark already. Last night the sun was still in the sky. I'm sure they're already finished.'

Arnetta acted as if she hadn't heard me. I followed her gaze with my flashlight, and that's when I saw the squares of light in the darkness. The bathroom was just ahead.

* * *

But the girls were there. We could hear them before we could see them.

'Octavia and I will go in first so they'll think there's just two of us, then wait till I say, 'We're gonna teach you a lesson,'' Arnetta said. 'Then, bust in. That'll surprise them.'

'That's what I was supposed to say,' Janice said.

Arnetta went inside, Octavia next to her. Janice followed, and the rest of us waited outside.

They were in there for what seemed like whole minutes, but something was wrong. Arnetta hadn't given the signal yet. I was with the girls outside when I heard one of the Troop 909 girls say, 'NO. That did NOT happen!'

That was to be expected, that they'd deny the whole thing. What I hadn't expected was *the voice* in which the denial was said. The girl sounded as though her tongue were caught in her mouth. 'That's a BAD word!' the girl continued. 'We don't say BAD words!'

'Let's go in,' Elise said.

'No,' Drema said, 'I don't want to. What if we get beat up?'

'Snot?' Elise turned to me, her flashlight blinding. It was the first time anyone had asked my opinion, though I knew they were just asking because they were afraid.

'I say we go inside, just to see what's going on.'

'But Arnetta didn't give us the signal,' Drema said. 'She's supposed to say, 'We're gonna teach you a lesson,' and I didn't hear her say it.'

'C'mon,' I said. 'Let's just go in.'

We went inside. There we found the white girls; about five girls huddled up next to one big girl. I instantly knew she was the owner of the voice we'd heard. Arnetta and Octavia inched toward us as soon as we entered.

'Where's Janice?' Elise asked, then we heard a flush. 'Oh.'

'I think,' Octavia said, whispering to Elise, 'they're retarded.'

'We ARE NOT retarded!' the big girl said, though it was obvious that she was. That they all were. The girls around her began to whimper.

'They're just pretending,' Arnetta said, trying to convince herself. 'I know they are.'

Octavia turned to Arnetta. 'Arnetta. Let's just leave.'

Janice came out of a stall, happy and relieved, then she suddenly remembered her line, pointed to the big girl, and said, 'We're gonna teach you a lesson.'

'Shut up, Janice,' Octavia said, but her heart was not in it. Arnetta's face was set in a lost, deep scowl. Octavia turned to the big girl and said loudly, slowly, as if they were all deaf, 'We're going to leave. It was nice meeting you, O.K.? You don't have to tell anyone that we were here. O.K.?'

'Why not?' said the big girl, like a taunt. When she spoke, her lips did not meet, her mouth did not close. Her tongue grazed the roof of her mouth, like a little pink fish. 'You'll get in trouble. I know. I know.'

Arnetta got back her old cunning. 'If you said anything, then you'd be a tattletale.'

The girl looked sad for a moment, then perked up quickly. A flash of genius crossed her face. 'I *like* tattletale.'

* * *

'It's all right, girls. It's gonna be all right!' the 909 troop leader said. All of Troop 909 burst into tears. It was as though someone had instructed them all to cry at once. The troop leader had girls under her arm, and all the rest of the girls crowded about her. It reminded me of a hog I'd seen on a field trip, where all the little hogs gathered about the mother at feeding time, latching onto her teats. The 909 troop leader had come into the bathroom, shortly after the big girl had threatened to tell. Then the ranger came, then, once the ranger had radioed the station, Mrs. Margolin arrived with Daphne in tow.

TOLERANCE, RIGHTS AND RESPECT

The ranger had left the restroom area, but everyone else was huddled just outside, swatting mosquitoes.

'Oh. They *will* apologise,' Mrs. Margolin said to the 909 troop leader, but she said this so angrily, I knew she was speaking more to us than to the other troop leader. 'When their parents find out, every one a them will be on punishment.'

'It's all right, it's all right,' the 909 troop leader reassured Mrs. Margolin. Her voice lilted in the same way it had when addressing the girls. She smiled the whole time she talked. She was like one of those TV-cooking-show women who talk and dice onions and smile all at the same time.

'See. It could have happened. I'm not calling your girls fibbers or anything.' She shook her head ferociously from side to side, her Egyptian-style pageboy flapping against her cheeks like heavy drapes. It *could* have happened. See. Our girls are not retarded. They are *delayed* learners.' She said this in a syrupy instructional voice, as though our troop might be delayed learners as well. 'We're from the Decatur Children's Academy. Many of them just have special needs.'

'Now we won't be able to walk to the bathroom by ourselves!' the big girl said.

'Yes you will,' the troop leader said, 'but maybe we'll wait till we get back to Decatur –'

'I don't want to wait!' the girl said. 'I want my Independence badge!'

The girls in my troop were entirely speechless. Arnetta looked stoic, as though she were soon to be tortured but was determined not to appear weak. Mrs. Margolin pursed her lips solemnly and said, 'Bless them, Lord. Bless them.'

In contrast, the Troop 909 leader was full of words and energy. 'Some of our girls are echolalic –' She smiled and happily presented one of the girls hanging onto her, but the girl widened her eyes in horror, and violently withdrew herself from the centre of attention, sensing she was being sacrificed for the village sins. 'Echolalic,' the troop leader continued. 'That means they will say whatever they hear, like an echo – that's where the word comes from. It comes from 'echo.'' She ducked her head apologetically, 'I mean, not all them have the most *progressive* of parents, so if they heard a bad word, they might have repeated it. But I guarantee it would not have been *intentional*.'

Arnetta spoke. 'I saw her say the word. I heard her.' She pointed to a small girl, smaller than any of us, wearing an oversized T-shirt that read: 'Eat Bertha's Mussels.'

The troop leader shook her head and smiled, 'That's impossible. She doesn't speak. She can, but she doesn't.'

Arnetta furrowed her brow. 'No. It wasn't her. That's right. It was her.'

The girl Arnetta pointed to grinned as though she'd been paid a compliment. She was the only one from either troop actually wearing a full uniform: the mocha-coloured A-line shift, the orange ascot, the sash covered with badges, though all the same one – the Try-It patch. She took a few steps toward Arnetta and made a grand sweeping gesture toward the sash. 'See,' she said, full of self-importance, 'I'm a Brownie.' I had a hard time imagining this girl calling anyone a 'nigger'; the girl looked perpetually delighted, as though she would have cuddled up with a grizzly if someone had let her.

* * *

On the fourth morning, we boarded the bus to go home.

The previous day had been spent building miniature churches from Popsicle sticks. We hardly left the cabin. Mrs. Margolin and Mrs. Hedy guarded us so closely, almost no one talked for the entire day.

Even on the day of departure from Camp Crescendo, all was serious and silent. The bus ride began quietly enough. Arnetta had to sit beside Mrs. Margolin; Octavia had to sit beside her mother. I sat beside Daphne, who gave me her prize journal without a word of explanation.

'You don't want it?'

She shook her head no. It was empty.

Then Mrs. Hedy began to weep. 'Octavia,' Mrs. Hedy said to her daughter without looking at her, 'I'm going to sit with Mrs. Margolin. All right?'

Arnetta exchanged seats with Mrs. Hedy. With the two women up front, Elise felt it safe to speak. 'Hey,' she said, then she set her face into a placid, vacant stare, trying to imitate that of a Troop 909 girl. Emboldened, Arnetta made a gesture of mock pride toward an imaginary sash, the way the girl in full uniform had done. Then they all made a game of it, trying to do the most exaggerated imitations of the Troop 909 girls, all without speaking, all without laughing loud enough to catch the women's attention.

Daphne looked down at her shoes, white with sneaker polish. I opened the journal she'd given me. I looked out the window, trying to decide what to write, searching for lines, but nothing could compare with what Daphne had written, '*My father, the veteran*,' my favourite line of all time. It replayed itself in my head, and I gave up trying to write.

By then it seemed that the rest of the troop had given up making fun of the girls in Troop 909. They were now quietly gossiping about who had passed notes to whom in school. For a moment the gossiping fell and all I heard was the hum of the bus as we sped down the road and the muffled sounds of Mrs. Hedy and Mrs. Margolin talking about serious things.

TOLERANCE, RIGHTS AND RESPECT

'You know,' Octavia whispered, 'why did we have to be stuck at a camp with retarded girls? You know?'

'*You* know why,' Arnetta answered. She narrowed her eyes like a cat. 'My mama and I were in the mall in Buckhead, and this white lady just kept looking at us. I mean, like we were foreign or something. Like we were from China.'

'What did the woman say?' Elise asked. 'Nothing,' Arnetta said. 'She didn't say nothing.'

A few girls quietly nodded their heads.

'There was this time,' I said, 'when my father and I were in the mall and –'

'Oh shut up, Snot,' Octavia said.

I stared at Octavia, then rolled my eyes from her to the window. As I watched the trees blur, I wanted nothing more than to be through with it all: the bus ride, the troop, school – all of it. But we were going home. I'd see the same girls in school the next day. We were on a bus, and there was nowhere else to go.

'Go on, Laurel,' Daphne said to me. It seemed like the first time she'd spoken the whole trip, and she'd said my name. I turned to her and smiled weakly so as not to cry, hoping she'd remember when I'd tried to be her friend, thinking maybe that her gift of the journal was an invitation of friendship. But she didn't smile back. All she said was, 'What happened?'

I studied the girls, waiting for Octavia to tell me to shut up again before I even had a chance to utter another word, but everyone was amazed that Daphne had spoken. The bus was silent. I gathered my voice. 'Well,' I said. 'My father and I were in this mall, but I was the one doing the staring.' I stopped and glanced from face to face. I continued. 'There were these white people dressed like Puritans or something, but they weren't Puritans. They were Mennonites. They're these people who, if you ask them to do a favour, like paint your porch or something, they have to do it. It's in their rules.'

'That sucks,' someone said.

'C'mon,' Arnetta said. 'You're lying.'

'I am not.'

'How do you know that's not just some story someone made up?' Elise asked, her head cocked full of daring. 'I mean, who's gonna do whatever you ask?'

'It's not made up. I know because when I was looking at them, my father said, 'See those people? If you ask them to do something, they'll do it. Anything you want.''

No one would call anyone's father a liar – then they'd have to fight the person.

But Drema parsed her words carefully. 'How does your *father* know that's not just some story? Huh?'

'Because,' I said, 'he went up to the man and asked him would he paint our porch, and the man said yes. It's their religion.'

'Man, I'm glad I'm a Baptist,' Elise said, shaking her head in sympathy for the Mennonites.

'So did the guy do it?' Drema asked, scooting closer to hear if the story got juicy.

'Yeah,' I said. 'His whole family was with him. My dad drove them to our house. They all painted our porch. The woman and girl were in bonnets and long, long skirts with buttons up to their necks. The guy wore this weird hat and these huge suspenders.'

'Why,' Arnetta asked archly, as though she didn't believe a word, 'would someone pick a *porch*? If they'll do anything, why not make them paint the whole *house*? Why not ask for a hundred bucks?'

I thought about it, and then remembered the words my father had said about them painting our porch, though I had never seemed to think about his words after he'd said them.

'He said,' I began, only then understanding the words as they uncoiled from my mouth, 'it was the only time he'd have a white man on his knees doing something for a black man for free.'

I now understood what he meant, and why he did it, though I didn't like it. When you've been made to feel bad for so long, you jump at the chance to do it to others. I remembered the Mennonites bending the way Daphne had bent when she was cleaning the restroom. I remembered the dark blue of their bonnets, the black of their shoes. They painted the porch as though scrubbing a floor. I was already trembling before Daphne asked quietly, 'Did he thank them?' I looked out the window. I could not tell which were the thoughts and which were the trees. 'No,' I said, and suddenly knew there was something mean in the world that I could not stop.

Arnetta laughed. 'If I asked them to take off their long skirts and bonnets and put on some jeans, would they do it?'

And Daphne's voice, quiet, steady: 'Maybe they would. Just to be nice.'

JUSTICE, CHANGE AND ACTION

DIVERSE SHORTS

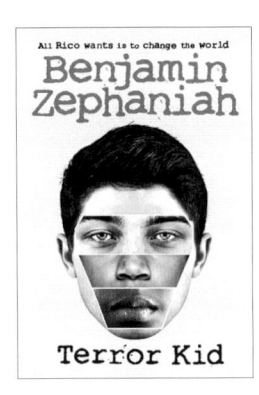

Terror Kid, by Benjamin Zephaniah

This extract comes at the start of a novel by Benjamin Zephaniah. It centres on the character of Rico and his reaction to riots in his home city of Birmingham and across the country. Rico thinks that rioting is wrong. However, thinking about the anger that caused them does make him ask important questions about what kinds of protest are available to people if they want to bring about real change.

Connecting to the topic

The three images on pages 73 and 74 were taken during riots that took place in London in 2011.

- How do you think different people felt during these riots? (You might like to write down the thoughts of a police officer, a rioter, and an innocent bystander.)

- If you were writing a short story about a riot, what message or messages would you want to get across? Why?

Connecting to the story

Imagine you are going to interview the writer Benjamin Zephaniah about *Terror Kid*.

- In pairs think of up to 10 questions you would like to ask him about the opening to the novel. Focus as much as possible on important details contained in the chapters you read, e.g. why did you set the start of your novel in the middle of a riot? Why did you want Rico to disagree with rioting? What did you want to suggest about the police and their relationship with young people?

- When you have finished your list, one of you should role-play being Zephaniah, while the other asks the questions.

- Write up your role play, either as questions and answers, or as a magazine article or blog.

JUSTICE, CHANGE AND ACTION

Connecting to the real world

- In twos or threes, discuss the extent to which you agree or disagree with each of these statements on a scale of 1-5 (1 disagree very strongly; 5 agree totally).
- Choose one statement you can talk about to the rest of the class. You should explain where you put it on the scale and why.

Rioting is a legitimate form of protest when people feel a powerful sense of injustice – they wouldn't behave like that otherwise.
Rioting is an excuse for violence, only carried out by those who are not able to develop their own reasoned arguments.
Those involved in rioting should always receive the maximum penalty (longest prison sentence, biggest fine) that the law can give to them.

DIVERSE SHORTS

JUSTICE, CHANGE AND ACTION

TERROR KID

BENJAMIN ZEPHANIAH

Chapter 1: Riot in Progress

Rico stood and stared as the shopping trolley flew through the air and smashed through the sports shop window. The boots and shoulders of the rioters had already weakened the toughened glass, and the force of the trolley caused the whole pane to shatter and collapse. Before the glass had even settled, a sea of people charged into the shop. The rioters danced, they chanted and they celebrated as they left the shop carrying balls, bats, trainers and football shirts, anything they could pick up and carry away.

It was a hot, sticky Friday night in Birmingham, but the riots happening there had started five days earlier when a young woman had been shot dead by police in Leyton, East London. Young people all over London were angered, and started protests and demonstrations. On one of those demonstrations a police officer pushed another teenage girl to the ground and kicked her whilst she was down. A bystander filmed it all on his phone and uploaded it to the Internet, and then the anger spread. The demonstrations turned to riots, and in a few days the riots had spread west to Bristol and north to Wolverhampton, Salford, Nottingham, Manchester and Rico's city, Birmingham. The British people, mainly young people of all races, all faiths, and many with no faith, were rioting up and down the country. They had had enough.

Rico Federico stood on Dudley Road and watched as shop after shop was smashed, rushed and then emptied. A large number of police wearing hard helmets and dressed in heavy black protective clothing gathered at the top of the road carrying shields. The police charged but they were outnumbered by the mob and were soon forced back to watch from their lines. A police car and a bus were set on fire. Fire alarms, car alarms and burglar alarms rang out from near and far, and Rico seemed to be the only one standing still. He turned a full circle to see the destruction all about him. Suddenly someone put their arm around his shoulders and ran their fingers through his hair.

'Rico, it's showtime,' a voice shouted in his ear.

It was Karima. Karima was the tough, fiery daughter of Somalian refugees and the closest Rico had to a best friend, but they were very different in character.

Karima was charismatic and had many other friends. Rico just had Karima. She was into kick-boxing and grappling; Rico couldn't beat a doll up. Karima was loud, cool and streetwise; Rico wasn't. Karima was addicted to social networking sites; Rico didn't care for them. But even though Rico wasn't interested in chatting to people online or collecting hundreds of online friends, he was definitely into computer hardware, computer programming and his computer repair business. He was really into computers. But to relax they both loved playing computer games. Karima just loved the thrill of winning, whilst Rico would spend time modifying the code and changing the graphics. They were an odd couple.

Rico was surprised to see her.

'What you doing here?' said Rico, looking at the gang of other people that she was with.

'Shopping, man,' she said with a wide grin on her face.

'Shopping?' Rico replied disapprovingly.

'The revolution has come, let's go shopping!' Karima shouted, beckoning him on as if into battle.

'It doesn't work like that,' said Rico, taking her arm off his shoulder.

Karima and her gang ran off into a phone shop to continue their shopping, and Rico began to walk away.

* * *

Everybody, it seemed, was doing something, either heading to a shop to get free stuff, or leaving a shop with their hands full. Some carried their loot on top of their heads, some on bicycles, and others used shopping trolleys from the very shops they had looted. It was so easy. The police were at one end of the street, but the rest of the street belonged to the looters, who just took what they wanted and left at the other end. As he walked away Rico heard his name being called behind him. It was Karima and her gang. They ran past him with their hands full of boxes and bags.

'See you later, brov,' shouted Karima as they ran off triumphantly.

Rico carried on walking up Dudley Road and before long he had left the rioting behind and reached the road where he lived. As he turned the corner a police van screeched to a stop. Four officers jumped out of the van and ran up to him, but Rico wasn't worried, he was calm and ready to explain that he had nothing to do with the riots. But there was no time for that; he was taken straight to the ground before he could say a word.

'Where's the stuff you took?' asked one officer.

JUSTICE, CHANGE AND ACTION

'I didn't take any stuff.' Rico's face was being pushed into the ground, his lips pressed against the pavement, making it difficult to speak.

'You're under arrest for theft!' yelled the officer.

'But I haven't taken anything!' shouted Rico as he was picked up and thrown into the cage at the back of the van. The van door was slammed shut. Rico was alone, and there was silence. Then the van drove off at high speed. It wasn't the first time that Rico had been picked up by the police for no reason. Rico could only think about his parents and the stress his arrest would cause them. They had worked so hard to get where they were now. Both his parents were Spanish Romany. As children in Spain, his parents had been spat at, beaten up and refused education. But they had been determined to make a new life for themselves. They came to Birmingham where his father had worked as a builder and then started a small building firm of his own. It was doing well but then they decided to have a family. Then he got work in the city planning department. He was quickly promoted so his rise from nomad to city planner was fast. His mother started her new life in England sewing shirts in a sweatshop, and then she went to college, studied hard, did her training, and became a nurse.

Rico's parents had often taken him to the library as a young boy and as he grew older he had read about the history of the Romany people. But he didn't identify himself as Romany, he was a Brummie; born and bred in Birmingham, with a Birmingham accent. With his straight nose, light skin and mousy hair, no one would guess he had Romany roots, not even other Roma people. He didn't smile much, he didn't hang out in gangs, he didn't follow the crowd, and he didn't care what people thought of him. Friends came and went, but that didn't worry him. He didn't use the word 'politics' much – like his parents, he didn't care for political parties, but he did care about people. In the library and inspired by his parents' lives he had searched out stories of how other people struggled and fought for their rights and of how sometimes people's rights were taken away from them. Like millions of other people he watched the news on television and saw wars and famines around the world, he saw how people were forced to flee their countries for safety, and how one group of people could oppress another, and when he had listened to all the politicians talking and making excuses, he still couldn't understand why. Why people did the things they did to each other, and why decent people didn't rise up to end the conflicts and inequalities in the world. He was sensitive to the suffering of others, but just feeling sorry for them was not enough: he wanted to help them, he wanted to do something. He was angry, but his anger was silent. He hated violence, but he wanted to change the world. He just didn't know how.

Chapter 2: Fire in Progress

The police van arrived at the station, and Rico was taken by two officers to the front desk. It was a busy night. Rico was waiting for the Enquiry Officer to process two people in front of him when he heard a commotion outside. He could hear officers shouting, telling their captives to be quiet, but they got louder and louder as they got nearer. Rico kept looking ahead until they entered the station and he heard his name.

'Rico. What's happening, bad boy?' It was Karima. She was grinning as if nothing was wrong.

'What kind of a question is that?' said Rico. 'Can't you see they've arrested me?'

'So what stuff did you get?'

'Nothing. You know I was just walking home and minding my own business,' Rico replied.

'You see,' said Karima, pointing to Rico as if he was a naughty boy. 'You should have done some shopping, brov, at least you would have done something to get arrested for.'

The others, three boys and one girl, all began to laugh, but Rico, not wanting to engage with any of them, just turned away and looked at the back of the boy in front of him.

'They're laughing, but even you know this isn't funny,' said Rico.

One of the many arresting officers now standing in the reception area shouted, 'Right, that's enough. Keep your noise down.'

Karima and her friends continued to laugh and snigger, ignoring the seriousness of their situation. Karima, as usual, was the leader of the pack and did most of the talking, working hard at giving the impression she was having fun. Rico always thought that Karima overdosed on fun to overcome the pain of her childhood. She had seen too much brutality of war in her homeland. But Rico didn't do fun. Outside of his family, Rico just couldn't find much fun in the world to be joyous about.

The Enquiry Officer at the front desk checked them in and they were all formally arrested, then they were separated and led away for questioning. Rico was taken to a room where he was told to sit down by the officer who had arrested him. The officer sat opposite him but said nothing for a couple of minutes. When he did speak he did so quietly, and slowly.

'Right, young man, listen to me carefully. My name is Detective Constable Holland. I'm going to give you a few more moments to think about where you are,

JUSTICE, CHANGE AND ACTION

and then I want you to tell me who called you out onto the streets tonight, and where you hid the goods that you stole.'

Rico wasn't playing his game.

'I don't need any more moments. I don't need anything from you. What I need is to go home, because no one called me out, I didn't steal anything, and you got nothing on me.'

'We got something on you all right,' said the officer, maintaining his low, serious tone.

'What?' asked Rico.

'We saw you walking down Dudley Road, we saw you talking to your criminally minded friends, and we know that you entered at least one shop on the Dudley Road and helped yourself to some stock. My colleagues are looking at CCTV footage as we speak, so soon, if you can't remember, I'll be able to show you what you've been up to. So you might as well tell me now. That way we save time and get this stuff done with quickly.'

Rico cracked a small smile. 'It's all good then. I can't wait to see this footage.'

'Good,' said the officer. 'I suppose you're now going to demand a lawyer and you're going to tell me that I should respect your human rights.' He pointed to the door. 'Well, what about the human rights of the people you're robbing out there? Hey, what about them?'

Rico was unmoved. 'I don't need a lawyer, and I ain't said anything about my human rights. I just want to see this footage you have of me.'

Another officer put his head around the door; Officer Holland saw him, and said, 'I'll be back.' And left the room.

Rico sat looking around the pale, empty walls for five minutes, then Detective Constable Holland returned and opened the door as wide as it could go.

'Right, pick yourself up, you're free to go.' He seemed to speak reluctantly, acting as if the conversation they'd just had hadn't happened.

Rico slapped the table and spoke angrily.

'You see. I'm sick of this. So where's this footage of me? There isn't any, is there? No, you lot just lost control of the streets, so you just start picking up everyone you can to make up for your stupidity.'

The officer stared angrily at Rico. 'What's this? You want to stay, do you? I'm sure it can be arranged.'

DIVERSE SHORTS

'I'm sure it can be arranged too, but whatever you lot do you can't scare me. Stop and search me as much as you like, arrest me as much as you like, you don't scare me,' said Rico. 'Give me my stuff and let me go. I don't need to stay here any longer.'

Rico stood up and followed the officer out to the reception. As they arrived Rico saw his father confronting the desk sergeant. His father was short, but he made the noise of many men as he stamped his feet, banged his fist on the desk, and pointed with his other hand, shouting at the sergeant.

'Let me in. I want to see my son now. You have no right to keep him here.'

The desk sergeant shuffled some papers around and replied without looking up.

'I told you, sir, we're bringing him out to you. Raising your voice will not speed up the process.'

'Process. What process? You don't have any process, you're just a bunch of crooks and liars. And don't call me sir. Now, where is he?'

'Here I am,' said Rico.

'Over to you, Sarge,' said the officer.

Rico's father, Stefan, shouted, 'Rico. Have they charged you?'

'No. They can't touch me,' Rico replied.

'You haven't heard the last of this,' said Stefan to the desk sergeant. 'I'm going to lodge a complaint.'

'You're free to do so,' said the desk sergeant, who then waved Rico over. 'I need you to sign for your possessions and you can be off.'

Rico's father carried on at the desk sergeant.

'You think you can do whatever you like? Well, you can't. This is the fifth time you've picked him up this year, for no reason at all. He's fifteen, what do you want to do, give him a criminal record before he's sixteen? You haven't heard the last of this. You wait. This isn't the end.'

Handing over a see-through polythene bag with Rico's belongings, the sergeant said, 'He was just in the wrong place at the wrong time.'

'The wrong place at the wrong time?' shouted Stefan, his voice getting even louder as he repeated the sergeant's words. 'The wrong place at the wrong time? That's what you lot say every time you pick him up. The wrong place at the wrong time. He was born in this area, he lives in this area, he goes to school in this area, and he keeps getting picked up in this area. So now you tell me, where is the right place at the right time? Come on, tell me.'

JUSTICE, CHANGE AND ACTION

'Come on, Dad, let's go,' said Rico.

Rico and his father left the station and began to walk home. The air was thick with smoke, the streets were busy, sirens could be heard all around, and tension marked every face. As they got to the bottom of the road a car screeched round the corner and sped towards the station. Rico and his father turned to look. The car came to a sudden stop. Two arms appeared out of the side windows, both holding lit petrol bombs, which they threw at the police station. One hit the police station sign, and the other landed in the doorway. The car sped away, going from nought to sixty in six seconds, and Rico watched as the flames got bigger. The steps to the police station were ablaze, flames began to cover the door, police officers ran out spraying foam from fire extinguishers. Rico turned and began to head towards the station. 'We have to help them, Dad,' Rico said.

His father grabbed his arm and pulled him back.

'No, Rico,' he said. 'They're taking care of it themselves. It's got nothing to do with us. We're just in the wrong place, at the wrong time.'

DIVERSE SHORTS

Looking for JJ, by Anne Cassidy

Connecting to the topic

The extract you are about to read is the first chapter of a novel telling the fictional story of Jennifer Jones, a girl who is found guilty of manslaughter when only 10 years old.

The novel explores issues around justice, the punishment of young people, and rehabilitation.

> Manslaughter: the crime of killing someone when the killer did not intend to do it or cannot be responsible for his or her actions.

- In pairs, discuss each of the statements below. Decide the extent to which you agree with each one on a scale of 1-5 (1 disagree very strongly, 5 agree very strongly).
- Choose one statement you can talk about to the rest of the class. You should explain where you put it on the scale and why.

Children don't fully understand the differences between right and wrong when they are only 10 years old.
Children should be punished under the same laws as adults.
Killing someone is such a serious crime that offenders should never be released from prison, even if they were children when they committed the crime.
A healthy society is one that believes that even the worst offenders should rejoin society after they have been rehabilitated.

JUSTICE, CHANGE AND ACTION

Connecting to the story

The Home Office is the government department responsible for matters of law and order. The story contains a fictional message from the Home Office about Jennifer Jones, which reads:

> 'Like any other offender Jennifer Jones has been carefully vetted. It was the considered opinion of all those concerned that she poses no threat to children and accordingly she was released under licence and is currently living in a safe environment. Any talk of revenge or vigilante action is wholly inappropriate and will be dealt with in the most rigorous manner.'

- Based on what you have read and your own thoughts, discuss in a small group how a writer might use a statement like this to develop their story. You might like to think about:
    - Why it might interest readers
    - The different possible storylines it allows a writer to develop
    - How you think this particular story will develop.
- Share your ideas with the rest of your class.

Connecting to the real world

Alice Tully reads about the Jennifer Jones case in tabloid newspapers. These use sensationalist headlines such as 'A Life for a Life!' and 'JENNIFER JONES FREE AFTER SIX YEARS: Is this justice?'

- Write down your thoughts about how newspapers should report on sensitive cases like this one. You might like to consider:
    - Whether they have a responsibility to respect the privacy of individuals involved
    - Whether they have a responsibility not to inflame public opinion
    - Whether the press have a responsibility to report what is in the public interest
    - Whether their main aim should be to sell as many newspapers as possible.
- Listen to a range of responses round the class.

DIVERSE SHORTS

LOOKING FOR JJ

ANNE CASSIDY

Everyone was looking for Jennifer Jones. She was dangerous, the newspapers said. She posed a threat to children and should be kept behind bars. The public had a right to know where she was. Some of the weekend papers even resurrected the old headline: *A Life for a Life!*

Alice Tully read every article she could find. Her boyfriend, Frankie, was bemused. He couldn't understand why she was so fascinated. He put his arm around her shoulder and dipped his mouth into her neck while she was reading. Alice tried to push him away but he wouldn't take no for an answer and in the end the newspaper crumpled and slipped on to the ground.

Alice couldn't resist Frankie. He was bigger and taller than her, but that wasn't difficult. Most people were. Alice was small and thin and often bought her clothes cheaply in the children's section of clothes shops. Frankie was a giant beside her, and liked to pick her up and carry her around, especially if they were having an argument. It was his way of making up.

She was lucky to have him.

She much preferred to read the articles about Jennifer Jones when she was on her own. It meant waiting until Rosie, the woman she lived with, was out at work. It gave her plenty of time. Rosie worked long hours. She was a social worker and had a lot of clients to see. In any case the stories about Jennifer Jones weren't around all the time. They came in waves. Sometimes they roared from the front page, the headlines bold and demanding. Sometimes they were tiny, a column on an inside page, a nugget of gossip floating on the edge of the news, hardly causing a ripple of interest.

When the killing first happened the news was in every paper for months. The trial had thrown up dozens of articles from all angles. The events on that terrible day at Berwick Waters. The background. The home life of the children. The school reports. The effects on the town. The law regarding children and murder. Some of the tabloids focused on the seedier side: the attempts to cover up the crime; the details of the body; the lies told by the children. Alice Tully hadn't seen any of these at the time. She had been too young. In the past six months, though, she had read

JUSTICE, CHANGE AND ACTION

as much as she could get her hands on, and the question that lay under every word that had ever been printed was the same. How could a ten-year-old girl kill another child?

In the weeks leading up to the ninth of June, Alice Tully's seventeenth birthday, the stories started again. Jennifer Jones had finally been released. She had served six years for murder (the judge had called it *manslaughter* but that was just a nice word). She had been let out on licence which meant that she could be called back to prison at any time. She had been relocated somewhere far from where she was brought up. She had a new identity and no one would know who she was and what she had done.

Alice fell hungrily on these reports, just as she sat coiled up and tense in front of Rosie's telly, using her thumb to race past the satellite channels, catching every bit of footage of the Jennifer Jones case. The news programmes still used the only photograph that there had ever been of the ten year old. A small girl with long hair and a fringe, a frowning expression on her face. JJ was the little girl's nickname. The journalists loved it. It made Alice feel weak just to look at it.

On the morning of her birthday Rosie woke her up with a birthday card and present.

'Here, sleepyhead.'

Alice opened her eyes and looked upwards at Rosie. She had her dark suit on and the white striped blouse she always wore with it. Her hair was tied back off her face, making her look serious and stern. Instead of her usual hanging earrings she was wearing gold studs. It was not the way Rosie liked to dress.

'Don't tell me, you're in court today!' Alice said, sitting up, stretching her arms out, ruffling her fingers through her own short hair.

'You guessed it!' Rosie said. 'Here, take this, birthday girl!'

Alice took the present while Rosie walked to the window and pushed it open. A light breeze wafted in, lifting the net curtains. Alice pulled the duvet tight, up to her neck.

'Do you want to freeze me to death?' she said, jokingly.

Rosie took no notice. She loved fresh air. She spent a lot of her time opening windows and Alice spent a lot of time closing them.

Inside the wrapping paper was a small box, the kind that held jewellery. For a moment Alice was worried. Rosie's taste in jewellery was a bit too arty for her. She lifted the lid off gingerly and saw a pair of tiny gold earrings.

'These are lovely,' Alice said and felt a strange lump in her throat.

'More your taste than mine,' Rosie said, looking in Alice's wall mirror and pulling at her jacket, using the flats of her hands to smooth out her skirt. She looked uncomfortable.

Alice got out of bed and stood beside her. She held an earring up to one ear and nodded approvingly. Then she squeezed Rosie's arm.

'You're on lates this week?' Rosie said.

Alice nodded. She didn't have to be at work until ten.

'I'll be home early. So I'm going to cook a special meal,' Rosie said. 'And it's not only your birthday we're celebrating. Next Saturday, you'll have been here for six months!'

That was true. Six months of waking up every morning in that bedroom, of eating in Rosie's kitchen, of seeing her name on letters: *Alice Tully, 52 Philip Street, Croydon*.

'My mum's coming. What about Frankie?'

Rosie had been making a special cake that had been hidden from Alice. Her mother Kathy, a funny Irish woman, was helping her.

'He can't come.'

She didn't bother to explain. Frankie said he felt awkward around Rosie, as though she was watching him, waiting to tell him off every time he touched Alice. He preferred it when they were alone.

'Oh well. It'll be just the three of us then.'

After Rosie left Alice sat on her bed holding the earrings and looking at her card. There would be nothing from her mother, she knew that. She sat very still for a moment, aware of her own body, trying to read her own sensations. Was she upset? She had other presents and cards. She had Frankie and her friends from the *Coffee Pot*. Then there was Rosie herself. Rosie with her powerful hug and no-nonsense manner; Rosie who smelled of lemons and garlic and basil and who was always trying to fatten her up. Dear, sweet Rosie. Alice hadn't known that such people existed.

The sound of the letterbox distracted her. She got up and took her card over to the mantelpiece and stood it up. Then she walked downstairs to the front door where the morning paper was sticking through the letterbox. She pulled it out, taking care not to graze it or tear the pages, and took it back up to the kitchen. Without looking she laid it down on the kitchen table and got on with making her breakfast. She tipped out some cereal and poured milk into her bowl. One dessertspoon of sugar was all she wanted. Then she got out the orange juice and poured herself exactly half a glass. Where eating was concerned she had a routine. She wasn't fussed about her weight or her shape. She just ate what she wanted and no amount of persuasion from anyone was going to change that.

She sat down and flattened the newspaper. There it was again, the headline she had expected.

JENNIFER JONES FREE AFTER SIX YEARS
Is this justice?

Her wrist trembled as she lowered her spoon into the bowl and scooped up some cereal. The story was the same as every other one that she had read over the last weeks. *Should Jennifer have been released? Should she stay in Britain? Is she a danger to children? Then there was the revenge angle: Would the dead girl's parents try to find Jennifer?*

As ever, the newspaper gave a brief outline of the story of that day at Berwick Waters. Alice read it. It was just like all the others. She had read them all. If anyone had asked she could have probably recited it by heart.

A bright blue day in May, six years before. The sun was staring down from the sky but a sharp breeze bothered the bushes and flowers, bending them this way and that. When it died down, the sun's glare was heavy, and for a fleeting moment it might have seemed like a midsummer day.

The town of Berwick. A few kilometres off the main Norwich road. It had a high street with shops and a pub and road after road of neatly laid-out houses and gardens. Beyond the small school and the park the road led out of the town past the disused railway station to Water Lane. A row of cottages, eight of them. Formerly owned by the council, they stood in a small orderly line along the road.

They weren't all run-down. Some were cared for, with conservatories and extensions built on. Others had peeling paint and broken fences. Some of the gardens were colourful and neat, their blooms in geometric beds, their terracotta pots standing upright, early blossoms tumbling over the edges. Others were wild with weeds and strewn with broken toys. Above them all were washing lines hoisted up into the sky, children's shirts and dresses struggling in the breeze one minute and hanging limply in the sun the next.

Three children emerged from a gate at the back of one of the gardens and started on the path to Berwick Waters. It was only a kilometre and a half away and they were walking smartly, as though they had some purpose. The lake at Berwick

DIVERSE SHORTS

Waters was man-made, filled up some ten years before by the water company. It was over three kilometres long and was surrounded by woodland and some landscaped picnic areas. The water in the lake was deep and children were not encouraged to go there alone. Some people said that families of feral cats had lived in the area and had been drowned when it was filled. At times, during the day, when there was absolute silence, some people said, their cries could be heard. Most people dismissed this, but many children were in awe of the story.

On that day in May the children were cold at first, that's why they were hugging themselves, pulling the sleeves of their jumpers down, trying to keep the niggling breeze from forcing its way inside their clothes. Five minutes later it was too hot and the jumpers came off and ended up tied round their waists, each garment holding tightly on to its owner. Three children walked away from the cottages on the edge of the town towards Berwick Waters. Later that day only two of them came back.

Alice Tully knew the story. She could have written a book about it.

She looked at her cereal bowl and saw that she'd eaten only half of it. She picked up her spoon and continued, chewing vigorously, swallowing carefully, hardly tasting a mouthful. At the bottom of the editorial there was a final quote from an official at the Home Office:

'Like any other offender Jennifer Jones has been carefully vetted. It was the considered opinion of all those concerned that she poses no threat to children and accordingly she was released under licence and is currently living in a safe environment. Any talk of revenge or vigilante action is wholly inappropriate and will be dealt with in the most rigorous manner.'

Where was Jennifer Jones? That's what everyone was saying. There were only a handful of people in the country who knew. Alice Tully was one of them.

JUSTICE, CHANGE AND ACTION

Orangeboy, by Patrice Lawrence

Connecting to the topic

This extract is about two characters who have taken the drug MDMA, also known as Ecstasy. The drug can give people a heightened sense of awareness for limited time periods, but can also make them feel anxious and agitated. It can have serious after-effects, with some people experiencing confusion, depression, sleep problems and anxiety for several weeks after taking it. It also carries a risk of death, particularly as it is often mixed with other substances that users are not aware of. It may also cause long-term changes to the brain.

The drug is illegal in the UK. Possession can be punished by up to seven years in prison. Supplying the drug can result in a life sentence.

- Write a paragraph or two exploring your thoughts about the inclusion of drug storylines in Young Adult fiction. For example, is it appropriate for young people to read about drug-taking? What types of storylines should be used? Why might a school want to use them?
- Share some of your thoughts around your class.

Connecting to the story

What are your feelings for Marlon and Sonya as you read this extract?

- In pairs, read through the extract carefully and identify 5-10 moments when you have a particular response to Marlon, or Sonya.
- Share what you think is the most powerful moment with the rest of your class.

Connecting to the real world

How do you think Marlon should be treated in the real world?

- Discuss each of these statement in turn and choose the one that you agree with most. Explain why you have chosen this one to the rest of your class.

Marlon should be arrested and receive a prison sentence/fine for taking Ecstasy.
Marlon should be arrested and receive a prison sentence for possession of drugs.
Marlon should not be punished at all for what he has done.

DIVERSE SHORTS

ORANGEBOY

PATRICE LAWRENCE

Chapter One

Man, I couldn't stop looking at her. When I closed my eyes, I still saw her. Her hair was thick and blonde, and a curl looped over her ear to her shoulder. She wore black mascara and green eyeliner and her lips looked shiny and sticky.

Sonya Wilson was right there next to me and it made my brain buzz.

The fairground was doing its thing around us. Every family in Hackney was out today, every eight-year-old in the world come along just to squeal at each other. The queue for the dodgems stretched out past the barriers and on to the grass. Legs dangled from the top of the Tower of Power as it shot halfway down to Australia and back up again. The Octopus was swinging screamers towards us and away.

All that noise was fighting with the music and the music was fighting with itself. It was the usual crappy mashup, The Beatles mixed with Frank Sinatra mixed with Michael Jackson. But underneath was a bass beat, thump, thump, thump. Like my heart.

What if I reached over and touched Sonya's chest to see if her heart was thumping too? Damn, she'd slap me from Hackney to Hawaii! I laughed.

She looked around. 'What's so funny?'

'Nothing really.'

She smiled. 'Yeah, it gets you that way.'

She finished paying for the hot dogs and offered me one. She'd squirted mustard and ketchup, an 'S' on mine and two straight lines on hers. I should have told her I hated mustard, but it was an 'S' for Sonya, like she was giving herself to me. My brain cells were glowing, all lit up with bubbles of serotonin. That's what Ecstasy does to you; it tickles your brain's insides. I grinned, at the hot dog seller, a steward, anybody.

Sonya said, 'Try it.'

I took a bite of hot dog and the claggy bread stuck to the roof of my mouth.

JUSTICE, CHANGE AND ACTION

'You like?'

'Mmph.'

I forced myself to swallow. A big lump of mustard dropped to the bottom of my stomach, bread and pink sausage churning up together. My gut jumped, ready to seal itself shut. Sonya was looking at me, so I took another bite and she nodded her approval. My brain circuits were flashing like Switchback lights.

'Better stuff it in now,' she said. 'When the pill kicks in proper, you won't want nothing to eat. Except, maybe me.'

I felt myself blush. She couldn't have meant that. Those South London girls must use words differently. She grabbed my hand and I was grinning again. I must look like Pac-Man. I wrapped my fingers round hers, not too tight or she'd feel them all sweaty. That must be the drugs again…

Or just being skin to skin with her.

We stood side by side, looking across the fair. Could she see it too? The world a bit gold and glittery?

I said, 'I think it's working.'

She shrugged. 'You only had a quarter, Marlon. But it's your first time, and the first time's always the best.'

Ha.

Maybe I should have kept my mouth shut. I could have been like Yasir or those other wide-mouths. If everything they said was true, they'd smoked their weight in weed by the time they were six.

I poked my tongue across the roof of my mouth. 'Should I have another drink?'

She rolled her eyes. 'You're all right. A quarter's just dust.'

It looked like I was heading towards sad-case country, so I took a deep, silent breath and put my arm round her shoulders, not too much pressure, keeping it all light. She didn't move away, but her arm stayed by her side.

'You're right,' I said. 'This is much better than revision.'

'Yeah.'

'My mum'll go mental.'

Sonya pulled her lips down into a sad face. 'You're going to tell her?'

'Course not!'

'So what's the problem?'

My mother's a secret god and she can see everything.

'Nothing. Look!' It was the pick 'n' mix stall. I still had a twenty in my pocket. 'Fancy some?'

'No. Let's go around before it gets really mad. You don't want too many people about if the pill sends you loony.'

I blinked. The world had turned dull again. 'It doesn't do that, does it?'

She gave a little sigh. 'I was joking! I've done it loads of times and I'm all right.'

Yes, she was. More than all right, but I'd be a slick creep if I told her straight.

I said, 'What do you fancy doing after?'

'I dunno. We haven't finished here yet.'

She sounded flat. I had to stop being so para. Girls like Sonya picked up on that stuff quick.

I smiled and said, 'Cool. It's up to you.'

But she must have heard something in my voice. She wriggled out from under my arm and moved round so she was facing me. Sonya's face was different from this angle and when she smiled, her cheeks were big and round like a young kid. She held my hand between hers and squeezed my fingers. Oh, yes! Now my whole head was one giant light bulb. You could probably see it from the moon, no even further than that. Thirty trillion miles away, an Alpha Centaurian astronomer was wondering about that bright new speck blazing through the Milky Way.

Her little finger moved up to my mouth and stroked the side. Thirty trillion miles away, a lens shattered from the heat.

'Ketchup,' she said. 'Seriously *not* cool.'

She unravelled her other hand from mine, took a tissue out of her little bag and dabbed my mouth. Even after she stopped, it felt like her finger was still there.

'Why think about later when we're here now?' she said. 'And even if we don't do anything after, we're definitely on for tomorrow. Today's like, I don't know, the starter. And tomorrow's the main course.'

Our fingers were twisting together again, black and white all mixed up. At least Mum wouldn't be funny about me going out with a white girl. Sonya's family might not feel the same way about me, though. I'd have to find a way to ask her. Not now. Next time, or the time after that.

JUSTICE, CHANGE AND ACTION

And Tish? What's she going to say when she finds out? She should be happy for me. We'd be equals.

I scanned the crowds. Imagine if big mouth Yasir or double-thick Ronnie were here. Or Amir or Saul, or any of them other idiots. I played it out in my head. They'd stagger off some ride and catch sight of me and Sonya. Their mouths would drop open in shock. I'd slip my hand out of Sonya's and slide my arm round her waist, all in real slow-mo. And we'd walk away leaving them staring.

I know that sounds shallow. And yeah, she turned heads, but there was more to it. I wanted to make her laugh. I wanted to touch her arm. I wanted her to know how my breath kept getting stuck when she looked at me.

'It's the Dizzy Drum!' She pulled me towards it.

'We've just had hot dogs!'

'So what? Come on!'

Say 'no'? Not happening. I just had to stop thinking about the chaos that'd follow if I threw up in there.

I handed the yellow tokens to the fairground guy and we went through. Sonya pressed herself against the wall and I moved in next to her. Our fingertips touched as the drum began to spin.

'Here we go!' She squealed.

I was slammed against the metal like a dead fly, my hot dog squeezed into mush. The floor fell away from us and Sonya was just a blur of screams and pink jumper. Our fingers slipped apart and now I couldn't turn my head to see her. She was shouting or was that the girl across from me? Or me? The blood was pumping through my head like it was looking to burst out. And that mustard. I swallowed, swallowed, swallowed.

It slowed down, then stopped. Sonya grabbed my sleeve, laughing.

'You all right, Marlon?'

'Yeah. Perfect.'

We stood there looking at each other, just for a second. Our hands locked again and we staggered off together, her shoulder nudged against mine so her hair brushed against my face.

If we have kids together, what will their hair look like?

Kids? I haven't even kissed her yet!

If I did kiss her now, she'd taste of hot dogs and fun. All I had to do was bring her towards me, put my other hand on her back and stoop down a bit.

She was looking at me.

'What are you thinking, Marlon?'

'Spaceships.'

How the hell had that been in my head?

She didn't run away though. She giggled. 'Why?'

I had to get this back, but my mouth had become an independent life form. 'The fairground. All the noise is like when the spaceship takes off. The flashing lights are when the engines go online and the gravity goes, and…'

Quick as it came to life, my mouth died.

'Er… right.' She stopped and let go of my hand, but it was okay. She was stroking my back now. The spine. Dead centre. 'They must have cut these pills with something really good.'

My stomach blipped, but I made my voice casual. 'Like what?'

She giggled again. 'Fairydust.'

I waited for her to walk away, straight on the phone to her mates about the moron she'd dumped in the park. But that didn't happen. Her hand worked its way up my back until she was tickling the hair on my neck. My follicles tingled, and my skin was straining up to her fingers like a happy cat.

And she said, 'Go on, Marlon. Tell me more about the spaceship.'

Kiss of life to my mouth. 'I know it's kind of geeky, but my dad was a Trekkie. Not just *Star Trek*, all of it, *Next Generation*, *Wrath of Khan*, everything. And *Star Wars* and *Blade Runner*, he was into that too. Even the really old stuff, like *Space 1999*.'

She stuck her fingers under my cap and twisted one of my plaits. 'Maybe everyone here's really an alien and we're the only humans.'

'Some people really think that,' I said.

She widened her eyes. 'Serious?' Her finger moved back down my neck until its path was stopped by my t-shirt. 'Go on, then!'

She was tracing shapes across the fabric, drawing circles on the knobbly end of my spine. Speak, Marlon!

She said, 'Come on! Tell me about all the abduction stuff!'

JUSTICE, CHANGE AND ACTION

'It's not really abduction. Some people have got this thing wrong with their brain, which means they never remember faces. It's called prosopagnosia.'

Luckily I managed to miss her with the bucket load of spit that came with saying that.

She raised her eyebrows, like she was impressed. 'So they don't recognise no one?'

'Kind of. It's more like they don't really remember what a face is. They think it could be an umbrella, or a hat, or, I don't know, a banana. So they might think their mum was an alien or something.'

Sonya breathed out heavily. 'Yeah, I can understand that. I sometimes think my mum's from another planet. How do you know all this stuff?'

'You know I told you about my brother?'

She nodded.

'When he was in hospital, the doctors gave me and Mum loads of neuroscience stuff to read. And then, I don't know. I just kept reading.'

'That's cool. Maybe you can be a brain surgeon.'

I laughed. 'How many brain surgeons do you know from Hackney?'

She poked my back. 'There may be some. Or you could be the first. You could really do that, Marlon.'

This was it. Now. With her face tilted sideways, looking at me with that smile. She had dimples! Why hadn't I noticed before? Perhaps she hadn't smiled this way before. My throat was all sandy and my mouth tasted of metal, but I could just touch my lips against hers. Starters.

I reached my arms around her and she moved towards me, like she knew the routine. She wouldn't let me if she wasn't happy about it. But she was happy, because her fingers were stroking my neck again. She was looking right at me. Around me. Behind me.

She stepped back, taking her hand away. My bare skin seemed to stretch out to her. I needed her to touch me again.

'Sorry,' I said. 'I thought you wanted to –'

'Not now.' It was like she'd put a forcefield up all around her.

I touched her arm. 'What's wrong?'

She shook her head and pulled away from me, stalking across the fairground. I stood there staring at the roughed up grass and rubbish. Was this a game for her? Had she got a mate filming this for YouTube? No. I was getting para again.

'Sonya!' I called. 'Wait!'

Her flash of pink jumper was disappearing through the crowds. I squinted. She wasn't by herself. There were three boys, brushing round her, much too close. One was a black kid with cane row. Him and a skinny white kid with a bike were on one side of Sonya. I reckoned that they could be the same age as me, but I didn't recognise them. The last one wore an old Stussy cap with his hood up, so the shadow made it hard to see his face. He was taller than the others, maybe a bit older. Then the black one turned around and stared right at me, a proper, hard screwface look.

What the hell?

It's her boyfriend. He's come for her.

I let my eyes drop, then looked again. He was walking away, the others sloping after him. Something far back in my brain started itching. Who was he?

'Sonya!'

I pushed towards her. All the dads out with their kids were looking at me, at her, then at me again. None of them were getting out the way. She was up ahead, standing by the Ghost Train, rubbing her face. Her eyes were shut. I stopped in front of her, went to touch her shoulder, but let my hand drop.

I said, 'Why d'you run off like that?'

She opened her eyes and stared right through me.

'I thought I was going to throw up,' she said, at last. 'But I'm okay now. It must have been that ride.'

'Those kids, were they hassling you?'

I know them.'

'Yeah, the black one, I thought I recognised him too.'

She shrugged. 'Maybe you do. I don't know your life.'

Sonya?

'It's just, I thought, one of them might be your boyfriend, or something!'

'You what? You think I pass between boys? You really think that?'

No! The words came out wrong!

JUSTICE, CHANGE AND ACTION

'Serious, Marlon! If you think that, you can just fuck off now. Actually, maybe it's best if you do.'

Her face was pale and she was screwing up her eyes like the air was too bright.

I waited a second, like I did when Andre went off on one, and kept my voice low. 'D'you think the pill's making you feel a bit dodgy?'

'No, Marlon! I don't!'

'Are you sure?'

'Just clear off and leave me alone!'

She was loud enough for people in the queue to turn around and look at us.

'Okay,' I said quietly. 'I'll go.'

But neither of us moved. Then Sonya jammed her knuckles into her eyes and her body hunched. When she took her hands away, green eyeliner was smeared down her cheek.

'I'm really sorry.' She rested a hand on each of my shoulders, with her forehead on my chest. 'I didn't mean to be such a bitch. My head feels like I've been shot between the eyes.'

'We can go somewhere quiet, if you want.'

'No, I'll be fine. It's sort of like a migraine and they come and go dead quick.'

Don't breathe too hard. Don't jog her head. Don't start her off again. Just –

I wrapped both my arms around her, breathing in slowly like I was drawing her into me. I closed my eyes and let my chin touch the top of her head. A massive group of kids swarmed past us, jumping around and singing the chorus to 'Thriller'. But it was okay, because I could hold her steady.

'Thanks, Marlon. I feel a bit better now.'

'Cool.'

'Do I look okay?'

'Yeah, great.' *Perfect.*

She grinned. 'You wouldn't tell me if I looked shit, though, would you?'

It would have been good to run through some of this stuff with Tish first. She'd have told me the right answer to that one.

Sonya was scrabbling in her little bag, probably looking for her tissue again. She glanced around quickly and pressed something into my palm. She was squeezing my fingers shut around a plastic pouch.

DIVERSE SHORTS

I looked down at my hand. 'What are you doing?'

'A present,' she said. 'We can share them.'

'What is it?'

She rolled her eyes. 'You know what it is. There's six there.'

Six Ecstasy pills, clenched in my fist. 'I can't take these.'

Her face clouded over. 'Why not?'

Because Mum thinks I'm at home with my nose in a book and she'll have a breakdown if she knows what's in my hand.

Because boys like me don't walk round Hackney with a pocket full of drugs.

Because...

'I just can't.'

She shrugged, then covered my fist with her palm.

'Aren't you enjoying this, Marlon? Me and you being together?'

'Yeah...'

'We can have a picnic tomorrow, if the weather's nice. Take another half each and just lie back and enjoy it. But it's okay,' she said brightly. 'I know you're supposed to be doing your revision. I don't want to get you in trouble.'

'Sorry. I just can't.'

She blinked two, three times, quickly, then smiled. One hand covered my fist, the other moved round my back, fingers pressing my t-shirt against my skin.

'It's not fair I take all the risk,' she said. 'If I'm a bit bad, you have to be a bit bad too. We can be bad together.'

Tomorrow, on a blanket lying side by side staring at the clouds, her blonde hair like sun. I'd lean over her and she'd close her eyes, reach up and pull me towards her. She was looking up at me again. Her lips were still shiny. If I kissed them, would my mouth be shiny too?

'Well?' she asked.

I shoved the pouch deep into my jeans pocket. I moved to put my arm around her, but she wriggled away.

'Come on!' she said. 'Let's go on this!'

'The ghost train? They're always crap!'

JUSTICE, CHANGE AND ACTION

Her thumb stroked the backs of my fingers. It was like pressing a lever; a dam opened and all my endorphins came rushing out. She moved her lips close to my ear. 'It's dark in there. You can balls it.'

'What?'

'The pills. You know, stick them down your pants. Make sure they're safe.'

How'd she know about that? I only knew because that was one of Andre's old mates' tricks. Sometimes they'd even wear two pairs of joggers to make sure their stash was good and snug.

I said, 'Yeah. Sure.'

I handed over more yellow tokens to a kid in a red jacket. Even he did a double-take at Sonya. I smiled right back at him.

It was a tight fit in the carriage, even though neither one of us was fat. The bar pushed down on my thighs. My jeans were rubbing against Sonya's, the pouch in my pocket squeezing against her hip. I was never going to get it out and in my pants here, not unless she was going to help me.

Jesus, Marlon. Show some respect! My brother may have worked his way round two local sixth forms by the time he was my age. But I didn't want *gyals*. I wanted one girl, this girl, sitting next to me. I'd risk the Portaloo afterwards and stash the pills then.

I rested my arm along the back, my fingertips in Sonya's hair. Just a few millimetres away, Sonya's head was full of thoughts. I wished I could see them.

The carriage slammed through the door into total blackness and the air seemed to wobble with the noise.

'Mum and Dad used to take us to Littlehampton,' I said. 'I was only four, but even then I knew the ghost train was pretty crap.'

She didn't answer me, but she probably hadn't heard. It was hard to hear anything with the mad volume soundtrack, groans and shrieks, rattling chains and banging doors, probably ramped right up to stop us thinking about how sad everything was. I peered into the gloom. Light flashed on and off grey witches with enormous noses and plastic bones the colour of old butter. An ogre shrieked in a corner and somewhere far back, a kid screamed. They didn't sound like they meant it.

But the light was weird in there, like they'd sucked every bright colour into a hole. I looked down at my hands; they were grey. Sonya's fingers jerked on the bar, then she relaxed back. I covered her hand with mine, the same way she'd done with me.

A zombie poked its head out of a hole and bellowed at us.

I laughed. 'Look at that one! You can see the strings holding it up!'

Sonya didn't reply, didn't even look at me. Maybe, and my chest hurt thinking this, maybe she really didn't want to be with me after all.

We bumped to a stop. I flexed my arm, my fingers catching for a moment in her hair. Still no reaction. I turned to her, but she was staring straight ahead. A fairground guy released the bars of the carriage in front. He was waving a severed head, making the little kids squeal. It was a rubber and plastic thing, with eyes that rolled up and down.

'Sonya?'

The severed head was coming our way now. What would she do if I just dropped the pills in her lap and went off and left her?

'Sonya?'

The fairground guy was standing in front of us, the head drooped in his hand. His lips were moving, like he was singing her a song.

'Sonya!' I nudged her shoulder. Her head slumped forward, her hands still gripping the bar. A smear of bright mustard blazed on her sleeve.

God…

Her neck was all bent over, not the way bodies should be. If I turned away, if I blinked long and hard, she'd sit up and laugh at me. This was her joke. It couldn't be real.

The bar yanked up, the men pulling Sonya from the seat, me trying to stumble after them. Strangers laying Sonya on the floor, hands pumping her chest making her body jolt around. A man's mouth pushing air through her – *shiny* – lips. The silence when the first aider leaned away from her.

And that kid with the cane row, just there behind the barrier.

No, all this must be a brain glitch, the Ecstasy tickling way too hard.

The shriek building in the bottom of my throat, that was real.

JUSTICE, CHANGE AND ACTION

Chapter 2

A bloke in a high-vis jacket had his arm round my shoulders, pulling me. I couldn't walk; my legs kept rolling away.

'Easy,' he said. 'I've got you.'

I strained to look back, past the wall of people, at the shape lying on the ground. A coat was spread across Sonya's chest. A man was kneeling beside her with his face in his hands. The woman standing behind him shook her head. And the kid with cane row – nowhere.

'Where are we going?' My words were lost in the sirens blasting towards me. An ambulance pulled up close to the ride, followed by police vans and police cars.

'You need to sit down.'

The steward had gone and I hadn't noticed. I'd been passed on to the coppers. The policewoman put her arm round my shoulders, gently, like the way I'd tried with Sonya. Her copper mate looked like he should be rowing a Viking longboat. He was scanning me up and down.

'What happened?' The words crumpled, but they must have understood.

The policewoman said, 'We need you to help us find out.'

They led me to one of those stalls where you throw a hoop to win a prize. Viking pulled together three red plastic chairs. I needed that seat badly.

The woman said, 'I'm PC Bashir. What's your name?'

'Marlon. Marlon Sunday.'

She nodded towards Viking. 'This is PC Sanderson. Marlon, we need to ask you a few questions. Before we start, do you need a drink? Water? Tea?'

'I…' The copper fizzed out for a second. All those lights across my brain had snapped off and I was in deep darkness. I gripped the edges of the seat to stop myself pitching forward. As I shifted, the pouch of pills pressed into my side, a proper 'here-I-am' poke. The police must be deaf if they didn't hear that.

'Marlon? Are you okay?' Bashir looked concerned.

Viking didn't seem bothered at all. If I collapsed on the floor, he'd probably complain about the trouble of stepping over me.

Sick joke. You're sitting here, alive. And Sonya…

Something heavy and sour was rising in my throat. I swallowed hard.

DIVERSE SHORTS

I said, 'Can I have some hot chocolate, please?'

Viking gave me an annoyed look, but Bashir smiled. 'I'm sure we can find some somewhere.'

She called over a yellow-coater. I looked across the park. The police had come quick; they must have been here already, checking out the crowd. I suppose they had to since that bloke got caught in gang crossfire in London Fields. Now, they were making themselves busy. One copper was talking to the fairground guy who'd had the severed head; they looked over at me and the copper made some notes. A load of them were cordoning off the ghost train, leading the people still in it out the other way. The kids must have thought it was part of the experience.

All the other rides were stopping and turfing people off, the crappy songs cut off one by one until the only loud voices were blasting through the megaphones, mixing with a new lot of sirens. The proper numbheads had their phones up so they could capture this moment forever.

That had been my plan for later, a picture of me and Sonya together, first thing I'd see when I woke up.

She'd been right next to me when she –

I should have rubbed her fingers to keep the last warmth. I should have stroked the hair back over her shoulder. Because life can't jump away from someone that quick, can it? Not so you can't reach it. In hospitals they bring people back all the time.

My fingers were ice cold now, my toes too, like the day had shoved itself back into January. But the sky was still bright blue with skinny clouds and I could see the tip of the moon.

'This for you?' A fairground worker was standing over me, holding out a plastic cup.

'Thanks.'

It was dark brown water, scalding hot and it tasted like chocolate toothpaste. It must have come from a sachet. But the heat and sugar made my brain focus.

'Just a second, Marlon.'

Bashir and Viking were being summoned over by another copper and they stood in a little huddle nearby. Viking stared at me over Bashir's shoulder. My brother, Andre, would have stared right back, disappointed if he wasn't offered the challenge. But I wasn't Andre. I turned away from Viking and dug into my jacket pocket. I wasn't under arrest or anything.

JUSTICE, CHANGE AND ACTION

They couldn't stop me from making a call. As soon as I hit eleven years old, Andre made sure I knew the rules.

I had less than a quid of credit left and a tiny bar of battery. Mum or best mate?

My fingers felt like they belonged to a drunk tramp.

Please, not voicemail. Please pick up.

'Marlon?'

Thank you! Thank you! Thank you!

'Marlon? Where are you? What's that noise?'

'Sirens. Tish, I'm at the fair –'

'Me too! But they're doing some idiot thing, closing everything down. I was having a crap time anyway. I was supposed to meet a friend, but he's not answering.'

'Tish?'

'Who d'you go with? Why didn't you ask me?'

'I was with Sonya Wilson.'

Silence.

'The one from school? With the big blonde hair?'

'I think she's dead, Tish.'

More silence, then a scream of laughter.

'Hilarious! Sick, but hilarious. It would have worked if you'd used someone else. Melinda, maybe, or Bryn. But Sonya Wilson? I'd have to believe that first.'

'Yeah? Thanks, Tish.' I hung up and tried to stand, but my legs still weren't working.

'Take it easy!' Viking Sanderson had finished his conversation. He sauntered over and leaned back on the counter watching me.

I sat down again. Bashir was talking to a paramedic by the ambulance. Behind those screens, they must have lifted Sonya on to a stretcher, taken her in and closed the door. I buried my head in my hands and squeezed my eyes shut, though I had to open them quick again. Sickly yellow was swirling through the black, Sonya's hair, the counters, the mustard smudge on her sleeve. I could smell it too, like old rancid hot dogs. My forehead prickled with sweat. I retched, but nothing came up. Viking just stood there, still watching.

DIVERSE SHORTS

Bashir came back as my phone started vibrating in my pocket.

Viking raised his eyebrows. 'Not going to answer it?'

I shook my head.

The coppers settled themselves down, Bashir leaning forward. 'What's your girlfriend's name?'

My girlfriend, 'Sonya. Sonya Wilson.' I took a little sip of minty chocolate.

'Any others? A middle name?'

I promised not to tell...

'I don't know.'

'Her date of birth?'

'I don't know.'

'Was she the same age as you, Marlon?'

'She's seventeen.'

'And how old are you?'

'Sixteen.'

Viking and Bashir looked at each other.

Viking said, 'Do you have her address?'

I shook my head. 'She was staying in Streatham, that's all I know. She's really…? Is she…?'

Bashir bit her lip. 'We need your address, Marlon. And a phone number.'

I told them. Viking even rang my number from his phone to make sure it was right. He sat back. 'What did you do to Sonya?'

'What? Nothing!'

'You sure about that?'

Pressure behind my eyes, my nose.

Not here! I can't cry here!

Bashir cut in. 'It must all be an immense shock for you.' She dropped her gaze for a second, then lifted her head and met my eyes full. 'Marlon, we've heard reports that Sonya was shouting at you by the ride. Is that true?'

I nodded, sniffed hard, and again.

JUSTICE, CHANGE AND ACTION

No. Not in front of the coppers and everybody. Not with all those idiots hovering by the barrier ready to get a good look.

I breathed in hard, held it.

Bashir offered a tissue. 'I think we should call your parents, don't you?'

I wiped my nose, scrunching the wet tissue in my palm.

'Your mum, Marlon. Can we have her number, please?'

I just about managed to stutter it out.

'Her name?'

'Jennifer. Jennifer Sunday. She's working today. At the library in Willesden.'

'And your dad?'

'He's dead.'

'Oh. Sorry.'

Everyone always was. Even though they'd never met him.

'Anyone else?'

'No.'

'So, Marlon.' Viking was never going to be the one handing out tissues. 'What did you say to Sonya to upset her like that?'

'Nothing! She had a headache!'

'A headache?'

'Yes.'

'Had she been drinking?'

'No!'

Bashir's pen was poised over her notebook 'Anything else?'

'Like what?'

I clenched my lip between my teeth. Bashir was scribbling hard. Why? I'd hardly said anything.

She balanced her notebook on her lap, lay the pen on top. 'Do you know if Sonya took anything that could have hurt her?'

Fairydust.

The pills must be calling to the coppers like Frodo's ring. Viking was right on the edge of his chair.

He said, 'A complete stranger tried to save your girlfriend's life. He was in the queue with his kid when he saw what was happening and he came to help her. You saw him afterwards, didn't you? You don't forget that stuff quickly.'

I knew that.

Bashir again. 'If Sonya took something that hurt her, you may have taken it too. You might need medical care.'

Viking was shaking his head. 'Think about Mr Ibrahim, Marlon. He has to go home and tell his wife that a young woman died in front of him. He'll tell her that he tried as hard as he could to save her life. Maybe he'll always be wondering if he could have tried harder.'

'We need to know what you know, Marlon.'

The coppers' eyes weren't moving off my face. My heart was straining so hard my skin must be one big pulse beat.

'It was nothing!' The words burst out of me.

Bashir said softly, 'What wasn't anything, Marlon?'

'She – we – took some Ecstasy.'

Now my hip was jumping with the pulse – six little beats in their plastic pouch. My fingers brushed my pocket and I jerked my hand away.

Viking narrowed his eyes. 'How much Ecstasy?'

I couldn't look at him. Anything else but him. My best Pumas, Bashir's sensible shoes, the muddy wheel tracks leading up to the ghost train and the ambulance with Sonya inside.

'One pill? Five pills? Ten?' Viking was almost shouting. 'How many, Marlon?'

'Nothing much! Just a quarter!'

'Just a quarter?'

'Yes.'

'You got the rest on you?'

'What do you mean?'

'Marlon!'

JUSTICE, CHANGE AND ACTION

The coppers looked towards the voice. I stood up, Viking just as quick. Tish was ducking the cordon, sweeping past the copper who was trying to block her way. She ran straight up to me and threw her arms around me My eyes were stinging and I had to swallow hard, keep swallowing, so I'd be able to talk.

'Jesus, Marlon! What the hell's going on?'

I tried to say her name, but just over her shoulder I saw two tall coppers striding over.

Bashir said, 'We have to search you, Marlon.'

Tish faced the cop up. 'What you on about?'

'Tish.' My tongue was thick with dry spit.

'Marlon?' Tish moved back from me. 'What's going on?'

'We took Ecstasy.'

'Who? You? You're kidding me, right?'

No. I wasn't. She could damn well see I wasn't. My body, my hands, everything was shaking. The coppers told me to turn away and I held out my arms and stood with my legs apart. I closed my eyes, but it made their hands stronger, patting me up and down like they were trying to clear away dust. The pouch squeezed against my hip. The patting stopped and their fingers were in my pocket, yanking it out. My arms were pulled behind and the handcuffs slammed on.

DIVERSE SHORTS

Every Man Dies Alone, by Hans Fallada

Connecting to the topic

This extract is set in the early years of World War Two (1939-1945). Otto Quangel meets Trudel, the wife of his son, also called Otto. He brings her bad news: that Otto is dead, killed fighting for the Germans against the French. Trudel does not blame the French, though. She blames the Nazis, the ruling party in Germany, for starting the war and for their disregard for human life.

- As a class, discuss whether you think all British citizens should be required to fight for Britain in the event of a war. What should happen to people who refuse?

- Discuss whether your responses would be different if Britain was a **dictatorship** rather than a **democracy**.

Connecting to the story

- Skim through the extract and find statements made by Trudel that show her determination to stand up to the Nazis.

- Create a propaganda poster for those resisting Nazi rule that includes some of Trudel's words.

- Share your posters around the class. Discuss what you think will happen to Trudel and Otto [the father] in the rest of the novel.

Connecting to the real world

Otto tells Trudel his bad news against the backdrop of a Nazi propaganda poster that shows the names of three people sentenced to death by hanging for standing up to the Nazis.

- Hold a class discussion around the following statements:

It is everyone's moral duty to always stand up for their beliefs.
It is everyone's moral duty to always stand up to evil.
The penalty of death is too high a price to pay for simply standing up to an oppressor.
It is understandable that people do not stand up to evil when to do so risks death.

JUSTICE, CHANGE AND ACTION

EVERY MAN DIES ALONE

HANS FALLADA

It was easy for Otto Quangel to get into the factory; getting Trudel Baumann called out to see him was a different matter. Otto worked shifts at another factory, but at hers Trudel was set targets about how much work she had to produce, so her every minute was accounted for.

Finally, he was successful, helped by the fact that the man in charge was a foreman like him. It's hard to refuse someone with shared interests; it's even harder to refuse someone who has just lost a son. Quangel had no option but to reveal this information to the foreman in order to get the chance to speak to Trudel. That meant he would now have to break the terrible news to her himself, just in case she heard it from the foreman later. Fingers crossed there wouldn't be any screaming or fainting. After all, his wife, Anna, had taken it pretty calmly – surely Trudel was similarly level-headed.

When she arrived Quangel had to admit she looked lovely, even if he only had eyes for his wife. She had dark, curly hair, laughing eyes, high breasts, and a pretty, round face that kept its vitality even in the factory setting. Her blue overalls and old, patched sweater couldn't take away from her beauty. Best of all was her general joy for life, which came through in her every step.

Otto found himself amazed that his son, also called Otto, could have paired up with such a girl. But then what did he really know about Otto? He must have been completely different to what he thought. He certainly knew everything there was to know about radios: employers queued up for his services.

'Hello, Trudel,' he said, holding out his hand, which she quickly took in her own.

'Hello, Father,' she replied. 'How are things at home? Does Mother miss me? Has Otto written? You do know I like to call in and see you whenever I can.'

'You'll have to come by tonight,' he said. 'You see, the thing is …'

He didn't get to finish the sentence because Trudel immediately rummaged around in her blue overalls and pulled out a pocket diary. Now wasn't the time to

109

tell her anything. He needed to have her full attention. So he waited until she found whatever she was looking for.

They were standing in a long, drafty corridor, with white walls covered in posters. Quangel noticed one over Trudel's shoulder. He read the inscription: *In the name of the German People [three names appeared here] were sentenced to death by hanging for treason. The sentence was carried out this morning at Plotzensee Prison.*

Without thinking, he took hold of Trudel by both hands and led her away from the poster. He didn't want to see her and it at the same time. 'What's the matter?' she asked, confused. Then her eyes followed his and took in the poster. She let slip a noise that could have signified anything: a protest about what she saw, annoyance at Quangel's behaviour, even indifference. Then she composed herself. Putting her diary back in her pocket, she said: 'I can't come round tonight, Father, but I can make eight tomorrow evening.'

'But I need you there tonight, Trudel!' Otto responded. 'I've news about Otto.' He sharpened his gaze and the smile vanished from her face. 'You see, about him, he's fallen.'

Strangely, the same noise that Otto had himself made when he had heard the news came from Trudel's chest: a deep-rooted 'ooh!' She looked at him with glazed eyes and trembling lips, then turned to the wall and propped her head against it. She cried silently. Quangel could see her shoulders shaking but could hear nothing.

What a brave girl! he thought. She was so devoted to Otto. Otto was brave too, in his own way. He never went along with those bastards, never let the Hitler Youth turn him against his parents, always refused to play soldiers and hated the war. The bloody war!

He stopped. Was he changing too? His line of thinking was almost like Anna's with her 'you and your Fuhrer!'

Then he saw that Trudel's head was resting against the same poster he'd just pulled her away from. He could still read *In the name of the German People*, but her head blocked out the names of the three hanged men.

He suddenly had a vision: of how one day a poster might appear on the same wall carrying his own name, along with Anna's and Trudel's. He shook his head. He was just a simple worker, who wanted nothing more than peace and quiet, had nothing to do with politics. And Anna just looked after their house, while a lovely girl like Trudel would soon find herself another boyfriend...

But the vision wouldn't budge. Our names on the wall, he thought, struggling to get things straight in his head. Why not? Being hung is no worse than being

JUSTICE, CHANGE AND ACTION

ripped apart by shrapnel, or dying from a bullet to the guts. It didn't matter how you died. All that mattered was finding out what it was with Hitler. Suddenly all he could see was oppression and hate and suffering. So many hundreds of thousands suffering. As if the numbers mattered. If only a single person suffered unjustly, and he could put an end to it, and the only reason he didn't was because of cowardice and because he preferred peace and quiet...

His thoughts tailed off and he didn't dare think any further. He was scared, really scared, of where such thoughts would take him. They would change everything about his existence.

To distract himself he stared at Trudel and the words *In the name of the German People* over her head. If only she wasn't crying at this precise spot. He pulled her gently away from the wall. 'Come away from the poster,' he said gently.

For a second she glanced vacantly at the words. Her tears dried up and her shoulders stopped shaking. Her expression took on a dark glow. She covered the word *hanging* with her hand. 'Father,' she said, 'I'll never forget I heard about Otto in front of this poster. Much as I don't want it to happen, perhaps one day my name will be on the same kind of poster.'

She stared at him. He couldn't tell if she really knew what she was saying. 'Stop and think for a minute!' he said. 'Why would your name end up on a poster like that. You've your whole life to look forward to. You'll get over this, you'll have children with someone else.'

She shook her head determinedly. 'I'm not having children just so they can be cannon fodder.' She gripped his hands in hers. 'Father, can you really carry on living like before, now that they've shot your Otto?'

Once more she looked at him with a penetrating gaze. He tried to ignore it. 'It was the French,' he mumbled.

'The French!' She was indignant. 'That's no excuse! Who invaded France? Come on, Father!'

'But what can we do?' said Otto Quangel, unnerved by the force of her words. 'We are so few and Hitler has many millions. Now he's defeated France, there will be even more. What on earth can we do?'

'We can do plenty!' she whispered. 'We can sabotage the factory, we can make our work shoddy, do it slowly. We can tear down these posters and put other ones up that tell people the truth about what is going on.' She lowered her voice further: 'The important thing is we remain different to them, never become them, or start thinking like them. Even if they conquer the world, we must never become Nazis.'

'But what will that prove?' asked Otto Quangel. 'I don't see the point.'

'Father,' she replied, 'once upon a time I didn't see the point either and I'm not sure I fully get it even now. But we have a secret resistance cell here in the factory, a small one, three men and me. Someone else came and explained it to me. He said we were like good seeds in a field of weeds. Take away the good seeds and only the weeds would be left. As it is, the good seeds can spread…'

She broke off, shocked about something.

'What is it, Trudel?' he asked. 'What you're saying makes sense. I'll think about it. I've so much to think about.'

She looked shamed and full of guilt. 'I've gone and told about the cell when I swore I wouldn't tell anyone.'

'Don't worry, Trudel,' he said, the calmness in his voice helping to settle her down. 'You know with me that things go in one ear and straight out of the other. I've forgotten what you said already.' He stared firmly at the poster. 'The whole Gestapo can turn up for all I care. I don't know a thing. And if it makes you feel any better, from this moment on we simply won't know each other. You don't have to come tonight to see Anna. I'll tell her something came up.'

'No,' she replied, her confidence coming back. 'I'll see Mother tonight. But I'll have to admit to the others that I told you and someone might come and call to see if you can be trusted.'

'No problem,' said Otto Quangel grimly. 'I know nothing. Bye, Trudel. I probably won't see you later. I'm hardly ever back before midnight.'

She shook his hand and headed off down the corridor back to work. She had lost some of her vitality, but still radiated strength. Good on you! thought Quangel. What a brave woman!

Quangel was left alone with the posters flapping in the draft. He prepared to leave. But first he did something that surprised himself: he nodded with grim determination at the poster in front of which Trudel had wept.

Next moment, he felt embarrassed. How over-the-top! Now he had to hurry home. He was in such a rush that he even paid to go by streetcar, something he normally hated to do.

DEMOCRACY, EQUALITY & RESPONSIBILITY

DIVERSE SHORTS

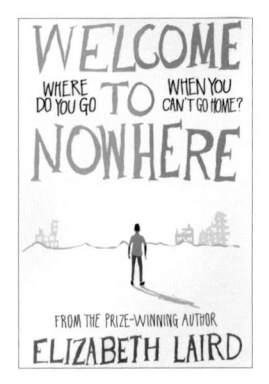

Welcome to Nowhere, by Elizabeth Laird

Welcome to Nowhere is a novel about a family fleeing their home in war-ravaged Syria for a refugee camp over the border in Jordan. In this chapter, they have just made the dangerous journey across the border.

The story is narrated by 12-year-old Omar. His mother and father (whom he calls 'Baba') are with him, along with his brothers and sisters. One brother, Musa, has cerebral palsy, which makes it difficult for him to walk. Two other characters are with them, Hassan and Yahya. They are not relatives, but young men who helped Omar and his family with their crossing.

Connecting to the topic

Welcome to Nowhere is based on the real-life conflict in Syria, where a civil war has led to millions of people fleeing the country and becoming refugees.

- As a class, discuss what you know about civil wars and about refugee status.

- Here are some facts and figures[1] about Syrian refugees. Discuss what you think about these figures. Are you surprised by them? Have they made you think again about refugees?

> War broke out in Syria in 2011.
>
> By October 2017 470,000 people had been killed in the conflict, including 55,000 children, out of a pre-war population of 22 million.
>
> 5.1 million refugees have left the country.
>
> 6.3 million people have left their homes but remain in Syria. (They are known as internally displaced persons, or IDPs.)
>
> The largest numbers of refugees from Syria are in the following countries:
>
> - 3 million in Turkey
> - 1 million in Lebanon
> - 660,000 in Jordan.
>
> *You can see where each country is on the map on page 115*
>
> Just over 8000 Syrian refugees have been resettled in the United Kingdom since the war began.

---

[1] Facts put together in October 2017, from https://www.worldvision.org/refugees-news-stories/syria-refugee-crisis-war-facts#fast-facts and https://www.refugeecouncil.org.uk/latest/news/5000_top_20_facts_about_refugees_and_people_seeking_asylum

DEMOCRACY, EQUALITY & RESPONSIBILITY

Connecting to the story

- In a pair, list the struggles of day-to-day life faced by Omar and his family.

- Together write a paragraph in the voice of the writer, Elizabeth Laird, explaining the emotional response you want your readers to have from this chapter and how you have tried to bring this about. You might like to focus on the way you portray particular characters, the way you describe the environment, and the effect of showing everything through the eyes of a 12-year-old boy.

Connecting to the real world

At the time of writing, 8000 refugees from the Syrian civil war have been resettled in Britain out of a total of 5.1 million: that's 0.15% of the total. In contrast, Germany has resettled more than 500,000 Syrians.

- Discuss the following questions in small groups and then report your thoughts and ideas to the whole class.

    – Does Britain have a responsibility to resettle more Syrians? If so, how many?

    – What is Britain's responsibility to refugees from other parts of the world (there are about 20 million people in total)?

    – Do rich countries have more of a responsibility to resettle refugees than poorer ones?

    – What is your response to Germany taking in so many refugees?

DIVERSE SHORTS

WELCOME TO NOWHERE

ELIZABETH LAIRD

Until we arrived in Jordan, I'd always thought of myself as being me: Omar. My father – Hamid. My mother – Leila. My brothers and sisters well, you know about them. I was Omar Hamid, from Bosra, then from Daraa, then from a village in the country, and my cousin was Rasoul and I was going to be a businessman.

Now, all of a sudden, I was a refugee. And even though my family was still there, nothing felt the same. We were at the bottom of the heap. We had only the clothes we stood up in, a few extra ones and a blanket or two (though Musa had brought his laptop, and Eman had smuggled in a couple of books). Nobody saw us as real people, who had had lives. We were just… refugees.

It was only later that all those thoughts came to me. As we came over the top of the ridge and saw the lamps set up under the trees lighting up some big canvas tents and tables with bottles of water on them, I just felt a wild surge of relief. Everyone else, all the people struggling up the path to safety, felt it too. Some were crying and hugging each other, and thanking God in loud voices.

We could still hear the occasional crack of a sniper's rifle on the far side of the ravine. The Jordanian soldiers (and there were quite a lot of them) had guns too, but they were slung across their backs, out of harm's way. And when they turned I could see the little red, green and black flashes of the Jordanian flag stitched on to their sleeves. I knew then that for us, the war was over.

One of the soldiers was talking to Baba, pointing him in the direction of the tents. Another had put his arms out to block Hassan and Yahya's way.

'No, no!' Hassan was protesting. 'That's our uncle, over there. Our family. We've come from Daraa together.'

Baba heard him, turned and nodded, a bit unwillingly, I thought. The soldier hesitated, but then another one nearer the edge of the ravine called out to him, 'Hey, Klef, come and help. There's an old guy with a wheelchair down there.'

DEMOCRACY, EQUALITY & RESPONS...

Hassan and Yahya saw their chance and hurried over to Baba. They picked up as many of our bags as they could carry and stuck closely behind us as we went towards the tents.

I don't remember much about that night. Someone gave me a bottle of water and a bread roll with some cheese. There was no room under canvas, but we found a place where we could stretch out together under the trees. It was quite noisy. Children were crying, and mothers were shouting at them not to get lost. It was cold too. I was glad then that Ma had made us sweat through the day in our winter clothes. I pulled my jacket over my head and went to sleep.

A kid tripping over my legs woke me up. I scrambled to my feet, fear kicking in my stomach, not knowing where I was. The sun was up and the light was blinding, but I saw the boy who'd woken me, sprawled out on the ground where he'd fallen.

'Oi,' I said. 'You should look where you're going.'

He stuck his tongue out. Then he picked up a stone and threw it at me.

'You little...' I began, and lunged for him. He darted out of my way.

'Riad!' a woman's tired voice called out. 'Stop that. Go and fetch water for your sisters.'

The boy took no notice of his mother but ran off to tease a group of younger children. The woman looked at me apologetically.

'I can't do anything with him. He's been out of control since they killed his father right in front of him. They...'

I didn't want to hear.

'I'm sorry,' I said hurriedly, and looked round for my family.

Musa was struggling to stand up. His muscles were always stiff first thing in the morning, but I could tell he was having more trouble than usual.

'You all right?' I called across to him.

He scowled at me.

'What does it look like?'

' Like something hurts?'

'My leg. Where I fell on it. Come and help me up.'

He hated asking. Before I could reach him, Hassan was hauling him to his feet. He glanced across to a Jordanian soldier, and I could see he was hoping that his closeness to Musa had been noticed.

Musa grunted something, which might have been 'Thank you', but probably wasn't.

Baba had walked across to join the jostling crowd of people clustering round a group of Jordanian soldiers, who seemed to be checking papers. Beyond them was a line of trucks with canvas roofs as well as a couple of ambulances. Someone with a bloody bandage wrapped round his head was being helped into one of them.

Baba signalled to me. I went over to him.

'Tell everyone to get over here. We've got to stick together now. When they've checked our papers they'll put us on a truck.'

'Where are they going to take us, Baba?'

He turned away without answering, but someone else said, 'To a refugee camp. To a wonderful new life. Five-star accommodation. Top restaurant meals three times a day.'

Amazing visions were sloshing round in my head.

'Really?' I said, my voice coming out all squeaky. I could feel a stupid grin spreading across my face.

'He's kidding, dumbo,' said Musa.

A soldier started to push at the crowd, herding people into an orderly line. Baba turned and saw me.

'What did I tell you, Omar? Get your mother. Quickly.'

I still get the shakes when I remember how Baba nearly left our papers in his jacket pocket in the stable house. With them, we could at least prove who we were. Without them, we'd have been lost in the desert without any camels.

A couple of soldiers had forced everyone into a sort of line and we shuffled slowly forwards. Hassan and Yahya hovered round us. Hassan tried to play with Fuad, who looked a bit withdrawn, and Yahya flirted with Nadia, in spite of Ma's discouraging looks.

'Overdoing it, aren't they?' Musa muttered to me. He was still suspicious of them.

We were waved through at last. Two of the trucks had already filled up and left and there was a panicky scramble towards the third one. Hassan got there first. He stood on the little flight of steps and blocked anyone else from getting on until our whole family was up inside the truck, sitting by the open back with our bags round us. I smiled at him. He seemed like a nice guy to me. The engine revved up noisily, ready to go, and a soldier lifted the steps into the back on top of our bags.

DEMOCRACY, EQUALITY & RESPONSIBILITY

'Help me, mister!' called a young voice. A boy who looked about ten years old, was holding up his arms pleadingly to me.

'Me too!' cried the little girl standing beside him.

'Where's your family!' shouted Yahya, above the roar of the engine.

'We're on our own,' the boy said, a desperate look on his face.

I leaned down, grabbed the little girl and hauled her in while Yahya lifted the boy. The truck was already moving. It lurched off with a grinding of gears.

It was strange to be crammed into such a small space with people we didn't know. I was annoyed to see that the boy who'd thrown a stone at me was in the truck with his mother and three little sisters.

'Stop it, Riad,' his mother kept saying. 'Don't do that.' But it was obvious that she had no hope of being listened to.

Ma kept looking at the two children that Yahya and I had pulled on board.

'Where's your mummy, *habibti*?' she asked the little girl, who stared unsmilingly back at her.

'She's dead,' the boy said in a matter-of-fact voice. 'Everyone's dead. A bomb fell on our house. We got out, just her and me. We ran away.'

'*Wallah*!' Ma's voice was soft with pity. 'Isn't there anyone left? An uncle or an auntie?'

The boy shrugged.

'We don't know where they live.'

He turned to look out of the back of the truck along the way we'd come.

There was no proper road at first, just a bumpy track across the desert. I had to hang on to one of the metal struts that held up the canvas roof and look out of the open back at the horizon to stop myself from feeling sick.

It was better when we turned on to a proper highway. It was silly, I know, but I couldn't help thinking about what the man on the road had said, about lovely restaurant meals.

I'll have the lamb kebabs please, I heard myself saying inside my head. *And some of those stuffed vine leaves. And the bread hot from the oven. With some baklava to follow, dripping with honey.*

DIVERSE SHORTS

I was so caught up in my dream that it was a shock when the truck pulled up with a squeal of brakes. And I was frightened, too, because I was staring out at a tank with a huge gun pointing out from the turret above towards a metal gate.

This is a trick! They're taking us back to Syria! I thought in a panic. *We're going to be in prison. Tortured and shot!*

Then I saw the Jordanian flag flying from a mast nearby, and began to breathe more easily.

Over the loud rumble of our truck's engine, I could hear the driver call out to the soldiers by the gate, 'I've got thirty-five in the back, more or less. Mainly women and children. Couple of young blokes you'll want to check.'

I didn't hear the answer.

I felt shoves from behind and a flurry of arms and legs. Hassan and Yahya were pushing their way to the open end of the truck.

'Thanks for everything, brother,' Hassan said to me quickly. 'We're going our own way now.'

'Where are you going?' Baba called out fretfully.

'Europe!'

Hassan had already jumped down, and Yahya was scrambling out after him. I was sorry then that I'd let Musa's suspicions influence me. I wished I'd been friendlier. They were only doing what Rasoul had done, after all.

'How are you going to get there?' I called out.

'Flight to Turkey. Sea crossing to Greece.'

A couple of Jordanian soldiers were looking at them, and one had started to move forward. Hassan was already walking quickly away, with Yahya almost running after him.

'If you get to Norway, and meet my cousin Rasoul, say hi to him from me!' I called out after them, but neither of them turned round.

There was the sound of a heavy metal gate being drawn back, and then the truck rolled forward. It stopped, and another gate creaked open before we moved on again. A short while later, we stopped for the last time and the engine was switched off. The silence was weird.

I heard the driver's door open. He came round to the back of the truck and reached in to lift out the steps.

DEMOCRACY, EQUALITY & RESPONSIBILITY

'Where are we?' Riad's mother called out.

'Za'atari. Za'atari refugee camp,' said the driver. 'Come on, get out. This is it. You're here.'

My stupid dream of a nice hotel and a wonderful meal faded away like a light going out as I looked round. The two sets of huge metal gates had shut behind us. They were shutting out the world of war, but they were shutting us in. To what?

I was the first to get out of the truck. Everyone behind me was so impatient I almost fell off the bottom step. I should have helped the others down with the bags and everything, but I couldn't move. I stood in a daze, looking round.

This is what I saw: long rows of dingy white tents, stretching into the distance, set on a flat, gritty, yellow, desert, dazzlingly bright in the morning sun. There were European letters in blue writing on every tent. I'm a bit shaky with the English alphabet, and though I tried I couldn't make out a word.

'*Unhcr*,' I muttered under my breath. 'Doesn't make sense.'

'They're initials,' Musa said behind me. 'United Nations High Commission for Refugees.'

'How do you know that?'

He gave me a pitying look and didn't bother to answer.

Everyone was out of the truck now, standing around, not knowing what to do. Suddenly, Musa staggered and half fell against me. I looked round to see that Riad had snatched his bag off his back.

'Hey!' Musa was trying to shout. 'Give that back!'

Riad danced around, waving the bag over his head.

'Cripple! Cripple! Come and get it!'

'My laptop! He'll break it! He'll...' Musa was saying desperately.

Um Riad saw what was going on.

'Riad, stop that,' she said weakly. 'Give the boy back his bag.'

Riad took no notice. I lunged for him with murder in my heart. Riad saw me coming, and hurled the bag into the air. I leaped for it and caught it, but landed awkwardly on my ankle, twisting it painfully.

'You little...' I began.

Before I could go on, Baba called out, 'Stop dawdling. Get our things together. We're supposed to be following that man.'

Musa had gone white. He held his hands out for his bag.

'I'll look after it,' I said, heaving it on to my back. 'And when I get hold of that imp I'm going to tear him limb from limb.'

It was all a bit of a blur after that. You realise, when you become a refugee, that there's no hurry any more. You might not be about to die from a shell blasting through the walls of your house, or a from barrel bomb falling from the sky, but you might easily die of boredom.

You have to stand about in line, waiting for someone to ask you a million questions and then give you a card which tells you that you're a nobody now. You don't belong anywhere any more. No one wants you. You have to wait in other lines, lots of them, until someone gives you a disgusting meal, which is supposed to be hot but isn't, in a greasy pizza box. And then there are more lines for vouchers that you can swap for a bucket, perhaps, or a thin grey blanket, a jerrycan, a heater.

At last, when we were all getting scratchy with hunger and tiredness, someone took us to our tent. We stood at the entrance looking in.

'Is this it, then?' said Eman disbelievingly.

No one answered her. Sand lay in eddies across the hardboard floor. A pile of grey foam mattresses was stacked up at the far end and the canvas walls billowed in and out in the strong breeze.

Ma said, 'Come on, Eman. Help me sweep out the sand.'

'What with? We haven't got a broom.'

Ma stared at her wildly.

'No broom! No nothing! All gone! Everything's finished!'

It was as if something had cracked inside her.

She ran blindly across to the pile of mattresses and collapsed with her back against them. Then she covered her face with the end of her hijab and burst into tears.

Baba looked at her helplessly. Then he turned on Eman.

'You heard your mother! Sweep the floor! Never mind 'no broom'. Use anything!'

Eman scowled. She tugged off her hijab and began to swish it across the hardboard, raising clouds of dust.

'Where are Hassan and Yahya?' Fuad said, following the rest of us inside.

'They've gone to Europe,' I said enviously.

DEMOCRACY, EQUALITY & RESPONSIBILITY

Ma lifted her head.

'And those poor little children!' she wailed. 'All their family dead! Where are they?'

'I saw them, Ma,' said Eman. 'A woman came up and took them with her. She looked nice.'

'They'll have special facilities for orphaned children,' Baba said dismissively. 'Omar, come with me, unless you don't want to have anything to eat for the rest of the day. We've got to swap these vouchers for a meal.'

It took ages for Baba and me to find the food place, and then we got lost on our way 'home'. We must have walked for nearly an hour, trudging up and down long straight tracks lined with identical tents, weighed down with a stack of pizza boxes and cartons of juice. I was beginning to panic when I caught sight of Fuad. He was standing out in the road with a look of horrified fascination on his face, watching Riad poking a stick at a little boy to make him cry.

'Baba,' he called out. 'Ma's upset. She thinks you've been arrested. Have you got any food? I'm so hungry!'

As we followed him into our tent I heard a familiar voice. Um Riad was standing in the entrance to the tent next door, calling out, 'Riad! Stop that! Come inside!'

My heart sank. We'd got the neighbours from hell.

While we'd been out, Eman had managed to get some of the sand off the floor, and had arranged the mattresses round the tent's sides. She'd opened the roll that she'd carried all the way from Syria on her head, and had laid a couple of blankets over two of the mattresses. She'd stowed our bags tidily in a corner, too. It didn't look like home, exactly, but my heart lifted a bit.

We sat down and opened the food boxes. We were all starving by now.

'They call this food?' said Ma, poking at a dried-up bit of chicken with a disgusted finger.

I was so hungry by then that I would have eaten a bowlful of mouldy rice. The meal wasn't that bad, but it wasn't nice, either. The rice was soggy, the chicken was as tough as leather, and the vegetables were squashy and tasteless. The best things were the hunks of bread.

I sat back when I'd finished my share, and watched the wind blowing in more sand, making patterns of it across the floor.

Eman whispered something to Ma.

'She needs the toilet,' announced Ma.

Baba wrinkled his nose.

'I've been to the toilets. They're disgusting. She can't go on her own. There are men hanging around.'

I knew what was coming and I didn't even wait to be asked. I needed to go myself, anyway. 'I'll go with you,' I told Eman. 'Musa, Fuad, don't you need to come too?'

Baba had been right about the toilets. They were in a breeze-block building that looked all right from the outside, but inside they were filthy. I'd never seen anything so disgusting in my life. Eman had to manage with her floor-length abaya, too. She looked pale when she came out, as if she was going to be sick.

'You mean we've got to go through that every time?' she said faintly.

I'd made sure to notice exactly where our tent was, but it still wasn't easy to pick it out from all the others.

'Omar, wait for Musa!' Fuad called out, when we were nearly there.

I turned round, and saw that Musa was limping badly.

'It's only a bruise,' I said, sounding unsympathetic even to myself.

'It's not. Hip. Strained it. Coming down the ravine.'

He held out his right arm to me. He didn't need to say anything. I knew what he wanted. I dipped my left shoulder so that he could hook his arm round my neck. We'd often walked like that before, ever since I could remember, in fact. I didn't mind helping him along. I was feeling quite shaky myself, and his touch was comforting.

'Thanks for getting my bag off that little devil.' He was wincing with every step. 'Do you realise they've moved into the tent next to ours?'

'I think he's funny,' said Fuad. 'He's really naughty.'

He looked up, his eyes going from my face to Musa's, reading our furious expressions.

'What are you looking at me like that for? I'm just saying.'

'That poor woman,' said Eman. 'She's got four children and she's completely on her own. Don't you feel sorry for them?'

'No,' I said brutally. 'If Riad's dad was anything like Riad, she's better off on her own.'

DEMOCRACY, EQUALITY & RESPONSIBILITY

Refugee Boy, by Benjamin Zephaniah

Connecting to the topic

In *Refugee Boy* Alem finds himself alone in London, even though he is under 16 years of age. He has been left there by his father, so that he can escape from the war between Ethiopian and Eritrean forces. He has no family and no friends to turn to.

- On your own, imagine that you have been sent alone to an unknown country to escape from a war. Write a few paragraphs, describing where you are, how you came to be there, your thoughts and feelings, and what you plan to do next.

- Share some examples of your work round your class. When you have done this, discuss what your priorities would be in this situation, e.g. finding shelter.

Connecting to the story

Alem is left by his father in a hotel, with only a letter by way of explanation.

- In a small group discuss how the extract presents the reaction of the different characters in the chapter to what has happened. You should consider:
    - Alem himself
    - The hotel manager, Mr Hardwick
    - Alem's father (through his letter)
    - The two women from the Refugee Council, Mariam and Pamela.

- Now, on your own, write a paragraph or two expressing your thoughts about how realistic this representation of the different people is.

- Compare your ideas round the class.

Connecting to the real world

- Imagine that Alem becomes a permanent resident in the UK. In small groups discuss how his future might develop over the next 10 years. Write notes for what you think he gets up to in two year blocks of time.

- Share your ideas round the class and discuss what the future holds for most people who arrive in the UK with no support networks.

DIVERSE SHORTS

REFUGEE BOY

BENJAMIN ZEPHANIAH

Alem has an Ethiopian father and Eritrean mother. Ethiopia and Eritrea are at war, so the family are caught in the middle and in danger. In the first chapter of the novel, Alem comes to London with his father, on what he thinks is a holiday. They do the usual tourist things on their first day in the city, visiting lots of sights. But when he wakes up the next day, as you are about to read, Alem finds that his father is no longer there.

After a long, peaceful sleep, Alem woke up late the next morning to the sound of people moving in the hallway outside. For a moment he forgot where he was. For the second time in his life he was waking up outside Africa, to the strange smell of full English breakfasts being cooked below. He looked quickly to his father's bed but his father wasn't there. He presumed that his father had gone to arrange breakfast and he wanted to surprise him by being wide awake when he returned. He jumped out of bed and headed straight for the bathroom, where he showered as quickly as he could. Soon his hair was combed and he was dressed, waiting for his father.

After sitting silently for ten minutes, he turned the television on. The news was on and he watched in amazement as the newsreader told of how a baby had been stolen from its mother in a shop, and of how a homeless man was beaten as he lay sleeping in a doorway in the West End. Before ending the programme, the newsreader smiled and said, 'And finally on a lighter note. The people of Tower Hamlets were the happiest people in the land this morning when the Queen visited a local factory to thank the workers for their service to the community.' Alem watched as the workers waited in line for the Queen to greet them. He watched their faces, wondering if these were really the happiest people in the land; he wondered whether the Queen would also visit the homeless man that had been beaten when she was returning to the palace. He knew that the palace was not far from the West End.

There was a knock on the door. Alem turned the television off with the remote control. 'Hello,' he said curiously.

'Hello,' came the reply, 'it's Mr Hardwick, the hotel manager. Can I come in and have a word?'

DEMOCRACY, EQUALITY & RESPONSIBILITY

'I don't think you can come in now,' Alem said nervously. 'My father is not here, but he will be back soon. I think he has gone for food.'

Ignoring this, Mr Hardwick opened the door to see Alem sitting on the bed. 'I need to speak to you,' he said solemnly as he entered the room. He went and sat down on his chair and continued to speak. 'Did you hear your father get up early this morning? It could have been while it was still dark – in the very early hours of the morning?'

'No,' Alem replied.

'This is a tough one, lad, I don't know how to say this but it seems that he did leave the hotel early this morning and he's left us all in a very awkward position.'

Alem was puzzled. 'Awkward position?'

'Yes, he left two letters, one for me and one for you,' the manager said, reaching out and handing Alem a letter still sealed in its envelope. Alem opened it. It contained a photograph of Alem with his mother and father, and a handwritten letter. Alem read it silently as Mr Hardwick looked on.

> Mr dearest son,
>
> You have seen all the trouble we have been going through back home. What is happening back there has nothing to do with us but we are stuck in the middle of it. You are the product of two countries, Ethiopia and Eritrea, and we love them both equally but they are pulling themselves and each other apart. We hope that it does not go on like this much longer but until the fighting stops and our persecution is over, your mother and I think that it would be best if you stay in England. Here they have organisations that will help you, compassionate people who understand why people have to seek refuge from war. We just cannot afford to risk another attack on you; we value your life more than anything.
>
> Your mother and I will try to use our organisation to help bring about peace but if we fail and we see no hope, then we may be joining you soon. If things get better, you will be joining us soon, but you must understand that we don't want to see you suffer any more, and we don't want you to go through what we have been through.
>
> We shall be writing to you soon, young man. Be strong, learn more English, and remember to love your neighbours because peace is better than war, wherever you live.
>
> Your loving father.

DIVERSE SHORTS

Alem held the letter and photo with both his hands on his lap and looked down in silence. Mr Hardwick looked around the room nervously, not sure how he should react. Then for a long moment they looked at each other before Mr Hardwick spoke. 'I have to say, lad, this has never happened here before and I'm not sure what to do. As far as I'm concerned you can stay here for two more nights, your father has paid for your room and all your meals, but you can't stay here for ever.' He looked down at the letter in Alem's hand, then at Alem himself, and spoke as if pleading. 'Your father says you have no family here – is this true? Don't you know anyone at all in England? Don't you have friends here?'

Alem didn't speak; he just shook his head to every question.

'O.K, well, the first thing we can do is to get you some breakfast,' Mr Hardwick said with a sigh of resignation.

Alem's breakfast was brought to his room that morning but his other meals were taken in the dining room with the other guests. He always sat alone by the window, looking out at the little pond and watching the birds that would come to feed from the bird table.

That day Alem went for a short walk, which took him around the small grounds of Datchet, the parish church of St Mary the Virgin and the town centre. The town was as pretty as a postcard. At its centre on grassland between two roads he came upon a stone monument. He stood there to read the inscription, ignoring the cold wind that was making his eyes water. It had been erected by the inhabitants of Datchet to commemorate the Great War of 1914 to 1918. It spoke of the glorious forces and their allies by sea, on land and in the air who had fought against the combined forces of Germany, Austria, Turkey and Bulgaria. The monument simply reminded Alem of war. Nobody is glorious in war, he thought as he walked away to admire other more positive items from the past in an antique shop across the road.

Back at the hotel, Alem sat for a while in the garden and then went to his room to watch television and read the guidebook. The staff and guests at the hotel seemed friendly enough and he was keen to know why Mr Hardwick called him 'lad' but he didn't have the nerve to ask. He would exchange a few words with people at mealtimes but apart from that he spoke very little, which made the day seem very long. Trying to learn as much as he could about British culture from the television meant that his mind was kept occupied, but every time there was silence he began to think about how he had got where he was. When did his parents have these conversations where they decided to bring him to England? Was bringing him to England really the best thing to do? Did they really love him or was this a plan to get rid of him? Would they care so much about his upbringing, his health, his education and then dump him?

DEMOCRACY, EQUALITY & RESPONSIBILITY

At one point Alem even began to believe that this was some kind of rite-of-passage thing, a test of manhood, an initiation test to see how he would cope with being alone and having to fend for himself. As he walked down the different hallways in the hotel, he began to try and peep into the other rooms to see if his father was hiding in one of them.

The next morning after breakfast Alem walked down the two miles of country roads to Windsor. He had read about the castle and thought that he might be able to see it, but when he reached the edge of the town he turned around and went back to the hotel. He was worried that he might lose his way in what looked from the outskirts like a much bigger town.

Back in his hotel room he sat on his bed watching middle-aged women have makeovers on breakfast television when there was a knock on the door. Alem recognised the voice of Mr Hardwick.

'All right, lad? Can we come in? I'm with a couple of nice young ladies who would like to have a word with you.'

He entered the room, followed by two women who both immediately locked their eyes on Alem.

'This is the lad,' Mr Hardwick said, looking at one of the women. 'Alem's been a wonderful lad, everybody likes him, no trouble at all – I wish there were more like him.'

Alem felt slightly uncomfortable. Everybody's eyes were upon him, which made him feel a little bit like an animal in a zoo. But when the woman spoke he felt different, much better.

'Tena-yestelen, Alem.'

'Tena-yestelen,' Alem replied.

'Ingilizinya tinnaggeralleh?' she asked.

'Yes, I speak English,' Alem said as he breathed a sigh of relief.

She was Ethiopian, she looked like someone from the Oromo tribe, dark, round-faced and slim. But what did she want? Alem wondered. Was she a good guy or a bad guy?

'My name is Mariam and this is Pamela. We come from an organisation called the Refugee Council. We heard that you were here and we have come to help you.'

Pamela was the taller of the two, white-skinned with cheeks highlighted with red blusher and short jet-black hair. Alem knew very little about the tribes of England but he was curious about the tribe that Pamela belonged to. He had never seen a European with a silver stud in her chin and six earrings hanging from each ear before. Still she spoke plain English.

'First of all we need to know that you're OK, and then – well, then we have to try and do whatever you need. We are here for you.'

'I think I'll go now,' Mr Hardwick said, turning and heading for the door. 'You three take your time now. I'm downstairs if you need me.'

The moment Mr Hardwick left the room, the atmosphere changed. Mariam and Pamela sat on the two available chairs and Alem turned the television off with the remote control, which was still in his hand. Mariam's eyes wandered around the room and took in the photo of Alem with his parents, which was propped against the bedside lamp next to his bed. 'So what is it like here then?'

Alem leaned back and rested on his elbows, now feeling more at ease. 'It's OK. The people are nice but the food is very strange.'

'What do you find strange about the food?' Pamela asked.

'Well, it's not too bad but it's very dry. I don't understand why they make the food so dry, and then they give me something called gravy to make the food more wet.'

Mariam and Pamela laughed out loud. Alem smiled with them. Pamela hadn't stopped laughing when she began speaking. 'You see, this is meat-and-two-veg territory.'

Alem repeated puzzled. 'Meat and two veg.'

'Yeah,' she continued, 'meat and two veg; one piece of meat, that's the centre of the meal – the centre of the universe – and a couple of vegetables thrown in for good luck. Oh yes, and a bit of gravy to help it go down.'

'Does everyone round here eat meat and two veg?' Alem asked, doubting the truth of what Pamela was saying.

'Yes – well, not everybody but most people. We are only thirty miles from London but you'll find that London is a very different place,' Pamela said as her voice began to settle.

'I know, I went to London and it was very different. So much people, so many cars, so many big buildings and I only saw the parts where all the shops were.'

For the next ten minutes they let Alem talk to them about his impressions of London and how he had spent his evening in the West End with his father. Soon Mariam thought it was time for them to start talking to him.

DEMOCRACY, EQUALITY & RESPONSIBILITY

'As I said before, Alem, we're from the Refugee Council. We know a little bit about how you came to be here and it's our job to make sure that you're looked after. We are not the police, we are not from the government and we don't have any special powers, but we are on your side.'

'We work with many people in the same situation,' Pamela interjected, 'so you have nothing to worry about.'

Mariam took out her notebook and began to make notes. 'We have to apply to what we call the Home Office for political asylum. We need to get you this political asylum status so that you can stay in the country. Because we want to make sure that your wellbeing is protected and you get the best of what we have to offer, we have to ask you a few questions to start with. Now, if you're having problems with English you can speak in Amharic if you like.'

'I will try to speak in English,' Alem replied.

'OK,' Mariam said while making notes in her book. 'Can you tell us what happened before you came here? What made your father bring you here, and what was life like where you came from?'

'Yes, I will try my best.'

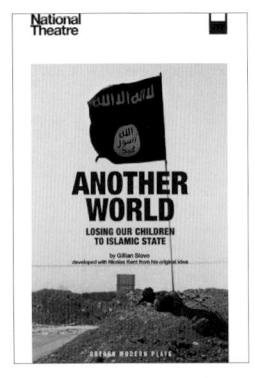

DIVERSE SHORTS

Another World, by Gillian Slovo

The extracts you are about to read are from a play called *Another World*. It is based on actual words of people involved with the Prevent strategy. This is a government initiative to stop people becoming terrorists, or supporting terrorism and 'obliges schools to report students who show any signs of being vulnerable to radicalisation to the appropriate agency'.

Those interviewed are all stakeholders in Prevent in different ways: from the young people it is aimed at, to those responsible for putting it in place, right up to the Prime Minister at the time the play was performed, David Cameron. One aspect of the Prevent strategy is to make it a duty for schools to promote 'British values'.

Connecting to the topic

- In a pair, come up with what you consider to be three important 'British values'.

- Share your ideas as a class. You should also discuss whether or not a value, in reality, can apply to a whole population.

Connecting to the story

The speakers in these two extracts represent different groups and interests.

- Discuss why you think each speaker has been included in the play.
- Choose one of the speakers you are particularly interested in and explain why.

Connecting to the real world

To qualify to work as a teacher, you must meet certain standards, including one to uphold British values, defined in the teaching standards document as 'democracy, the rule of law, individual liberty and mutual respect and tolerance of different faiths and beliefs'.

- In a small group, write a manifesto for your school about how it will actively promote all of these things. You might like to take one point each (e.g. one of you takes democracy, one individual liberty, and so on).

- Present your manifesto to the rest of the class.

DEMOCRACY, EQUALITY & RESPONSIBILITY

ANOTHER WORLD

GILLIAN SLOVO

Extract 1

Male D:	David Cameron, you know. Recently he said that British Muslim women have to, erm, learn English or, erm, face, erm, deportation. He's really alienating and just focusing on one ethnic minority and one particular group.
Female C:	Why is it just Muslim women? Why can't it be all? And why women? Why can't it be everyone?
Male A:	Someone says the word 'terrorist', it's almost like automatically in your head the word 'Muslim' comes before it, because the media, esp – newspapers and the TV, usually [use] the tag of 'Muslim terrorist' or erm 'Muslim man does this', but when it comes to other people, there isn't that tag. It's – yeah – it'll be, like, 'Oh, a man just does this,' or erm 'A rapist does this'.
Female C:	Sometimes I wear, wear skirts; sometimes I wear jeans. Sometimes when I'm wearing skirts I feel worried that people think, oh, that girl was forced into wearing that. And that kind of makes me think about my actions and – makes me think, oh, actually maybe I shouldn't [or], maybe I should just [to] prove to people that I can do this. I think that's happened to a lot of young people nowadays, cos they feel like they have to act in a certain

DIVERSE SHORTS

	way to show people that I'm not an extremist. Like [after], all these young people, especially the girls that went from Tower Hamlets, I feel as if now because it's hit so close to me, I feel as if I have to just prove [I'm not an extremist].
Female B:	Sometimes when I go on the train I have people literally, just stare at me for a very long time and that kind of paranoia is, what is there to stare at? Because there's other people in the carriage and you are only staring at me and that makes me think, is it 'cos of the way I'm dressing or like, is it because I'm wearing like a hijab or something?
Male A:	There are some words in, in public, like say, 'explode' or 'explosion' – I could be on the tube and I could be talking to somebody next to me about a firework show and be like, 'A firework went up and it exploded' but I would be really cautious of who heard it. Or I would just completely avoid the subject of mentioning anything like that, because people automatically they'll turn and they'll look, 'Oh, have you got a bag on you, are your pockets a little bit bulging?' or something like that.
Female C:	Yeah.
Male D:	I feel like the same. Like like sometimes if I just have to like put my bag down to like fix my jacket and suddenly I just have all these faces like turning at me and I feel like kind of like 'I'm not doing anything, I'm just putting my bag down to fix my jacket!' and I think, like, there's a paranoia around it.

Extract 2

Mohammed Akunjee:	Since 2000 there's been a number of changes in the law particularly the Terrorism Act 2000 and 2006 [which] have extended or created offences which simply didn't exist before in the UK, unless you go back to sort of Oliver Cromwell's time where we have ideas of thought crime or it being illegal to um own books or material that to a a prosecutor's mind would be relevant to terrorists

DEMOCRACY, EQUALITY & RESPONSIBILITY

or terrorism. And terrorists and terrorism have a very much wider sort of definition [nowadays]. Um and it encompasses things like having information likely to be of use to terrorists. Um that can include theological books. It can include um treatises on a religious discourse or... or l... legal discourse. It never ever says that it's specifically for the Muslim faith, that would be discriminatory in itself. Um but the law provides enough discretion and the practice of it shows that it is almost exclusively towards the Muslim community.

Human beings can deal with being told you can't say something, what they can't deal with very well, and rightly so, is where they feel that it's un... there's a lack of justice or lack of fair play. Britain has always prided itself on its sense of fair play and balance. And that's its core values, core principles. And I think we've lost our way.

David Cameron:
(Prime Minister's speech at Ninestiles School in Birmingham on July 10th 2015)

We are all British. We respect democracy and the rule of law. We believe in freedom of speech, freedom of the press, freedom of worship, equal rights regardless of race, sex, sexuality or faith.

Female B: [Those values] are shared all around the world. Why do we have to put a label on it that this is British. It's human rights.

Female C: While they're trying to enforce something that's supposed to make us more united, it's making us feel more segregated. The idea of British values is kind of playing on, Oh, okay, I'm [don't] feel a part of these British values, I've got – I've got erm Muslim values as well, or I've got Bengali or Somalian values as well. Maybe I should go join Muslim values in a different country.

Male D: I think subliminally [talk of British values] is having problems with the younger people. Me, when I'm doing erm – what are they called – questionnaires and the nationality part comes up, I don't know if I should tick the Bengali box or the British Bengali box or the British box. I don't know what I am because, am I British, so am

DIVERSE SHORTS

I like denying my Bengali background? Or if I'm British Bengali, would the British not accept me because I'm saying 'I'm half half'. Like, is there such a thing as dual nationality?

Moazzam Begg: David Cameron [made that speech] ironically in the school, erm that my son goes to – that son was born while I was in Guantanamo[1], while I was being interrogated by British intelligence agents – he came to that school and he gave a talk about extremism. And he gave points about what he said extremism is. And one of them is a refusal to accept democracy. Another is to be intolerant of other people's beliefs. Another he said was the rejection of the rule of law.

How many people in this country since the beginning of the war on terror either directly or indirectly have been renditioned[2], have been falsely imprisoned, have been tortured, with British complicity? Where's the rule of law there?

Prevent [the government's programme to stop extremism and radicalisation], prior to this was a voluntary thing. If you felt someone was radicalised you could contact Prevent officers and get them into a Channel programme [which is individually tailored to help them]. Now as a result of the Counter Terrorism and Security Act 2015, Prevent is law. If you're a professor at university or a lecturer or a doctor or a nurse, if you see somebody who you think is becoming radicalised, then you're obliged to report it to the Prevent officers, i.e. the police.

Charles Farr:
(Former Director General of the Office of Security and Counter terrorism and current Chair of the Joint Intelligence Committee which sits in the Cabinet Office)

It's not Police-led. I mean... a very wide range of statutory organisations very far from policing are themselves involved in Prevent uh, in their own way, not according to instructions issued to them by local Policing. Of course, the Police have to be involved because many Prevent Programmes are of … are of relevance to the

---

1 Guantanamo is a U.S. naval base on the coast of Cuba, where thousands of terrorist suspects have been detained, sometimes illegally.
2 Rendition is the practice of sending a foreign criminal or terrorist suspect covertly to be interrogated in a country with less rigorous regulations for the humane treatment of prisoners.

DEMOCRACY, EQUALITY & RESPONSIBILITY

Police and Police information needs to be used to inform Prevent Programmes because the Police will have arrested people who, uh, um, whose … whose history is relevant to the way we do Prevent So we need to understand and get information about and from the Police to ensure that Prevent is doing what it should do which is to stop the radicalisation of the people in this country.

Prevent is fundamentally about protecting those people. If they go to Syria and Iraq, they will almost certainly be killed, and before they're killed, they will be treated in a way that no one would wish on anyone and it seems to me that is what Prevent is doing, is trying to stop, and I have yet to hear what the alternative is. Does the State leave people to get groomed by organisations online or offline and encouraged to go to Syria? Does the State stand back and say, 'That is their responsibility, it is up to them whether they wish to go and get themselves killed?'

Really? I don't think, you know, in my experience, that's the view of most Muslim communities.

Mohammed Akunjee: We are supposed to be a pluralist society which allows freedom of thought and expression. The legitimacy of those ideas are tested by our reaction to people who speak things that we don't agree with and maybe are repugnant. I think we're in a very dangerous time when we're talking about the censorship of… of… of non-normative ideas.

One of the seven factors [in the Prevent strategy] is that you know men start, or boys start growing beards and women start wearing hijabs. The problem with that is that girls start wearing hijabs just out of religious conservatism at the age of puberty.

It… it… it's simply not a factor that helps anyone understand whether someone's been radicalised or not.

Shiraz Maher: The [current] Prevent strategy is bolder, it's smarter, it's wiser in some aspects [than the] Labour one [but] what they've given with one hand they've taken away with the other. The Terrorism Act was drafted deliberately vaguely because it needs to be malleable to events. And I think Prevent operates in the same way but the point is that's not a model that society should operate on. They are sort of getting to a result of pre-crime, getting into thought policing.

DAC Ball: You know, one of the reasons why people have concerns about Prevent is because they only see... visibly see police operating that area, so they assume it's criminalising and it isn't.

It's not [police led]. [Teachers] can simply draw support from the Department for Education, for example, um, or within their own school, um, to deal with whatever it is they're seeing. Um, there's no reason to bring it to police unless they feel that they, ah, they need to.

It's not just about extreme ideas, it's about violence, um, aggression, anger, um, and it can be that somebody's being abused by being radicalised in that way by somebody else. So, I think there are enough similarities for us to work within safeguarding procedures.

POWER, FREEDOM AND CONTROL

DIVERSE SHORTS

The Hate U Give, by Angie Thomas

The Hate U Give is a novel loosely based on the Black Lives Matter movement in the United States. This is a movement that campaigns against the unjust treatment of black people by the police in the U.S., particularly young black men, who are statistically more likely than other Americans to be shot dead by police.

Connecting to the topic

- In small groups discuss your responses to these three statements:

1.	People should respect the police at all times, whatever the situation.
2.	All police in the UK should carry guns. (The majority don't.)
3.	The law should apply differently to the police than to the rest of the population.

- Choose one of the statements and explain what you think about it to the rest of the class.

Connecting to the story

- Write two brief accounts of what you have just read from two different perspectives:
    1. From the point of view of another police officer watching on.
    2. From the point of view of a passer-by who saw the whole thing.

- Write down your thoughts about Khalil's behaviour. For example, was he justified in behaving as he did?

Connecting to the real world

- Write down your thoughts about whether or not you think the incident you have just read could happen in this way in the real world, with reasons.

- Write down your thoughts about whether the police officer involved in this chapter should be treated as a criminal in any investigation. If he is found guilty of an offence, what should his punishment be?

- Share your thoughts round the class.

POWER, FREEDOM AND CONTROL

THE HATE U GIVE

ANGIE THOMAS

When I was twelve, my parents had two talks with me.

One was the usual birds and bees. Well, I didn't really get the usual version. My mom, Lisa, is a registered nurse, and she told me what went where, and what didn't need to go here, there, or any damn where till I'm grown. Back then, I doubted anything was going anywhere anyway. While all the other girls sprouted breasts between sixth and seventh grade, my chest was as flat as my back.

The other talk was about what to do if a cop stopped me.

Momma fussed and told Daddy I was too young for that. He argued that I wasn't too young to get arrested or shot.

'Starr-Starr, you do whatever they tell you to do,' he said. 'Keep your hands visible. Don't make any sudden moves. Only speak when they speak to you.'

I knew it must've been serious. Daddy has the biggest mouth of anybody I know, and if he said to be quiet, I needed to be quiet.

I hope somebody had the talk with Khalil.

He cusses under his breath, turns Tupac down, and manoeuvres the Impala to the side of the street. We're on Carnation where most of the houses are abandoned and half the streetlights are busted. Nobody around but us and the cop.

Khalil turns the ignition off. 'Wonder what this fool wants.'

The officer parks and puts his brights on. I blink to keep from being blinded.

I remember something else Daddy said. *If you're with somebody, you better hope they don't have nothing on them, or both of y'all going down.*

'K, you don't have anything in the car, do you?' I ask.

He watches the cop in his side mirror. 'Nah.'

The officer approaches the driver's door and taps the window. Khalil cranks the handle to roll it down. As if we aren't blinded enough, the officer beams his flashlight in our faces.

'Licence, registration, and proof of insurance.'

Khalil breaks a rule – he doesn't do what the cop wants. 'What you pull us over for?'

'Licence, registration, and proof of insurance.'

'I said what you pull us over for?'

'Khalil,' I plead. 'Do what he said.'

Khalil groans and takes his wallet out. The officer follows his movements with the flashlight.

My heart pounds loudly, but Daddy's instructions echo in my head: *Get a good look at the cop's face. If you can remember his badge number, that's even better.*

With the flashlight following Khalil's hands, I make out the numbers on the badge – one-fifteen. He's white, midthirties to early forties, has a brown buzz cut and a thin scar over his top lip.

Khalil hands the officer his papers and licence.

One-Fifteen looks over them. 'Where are you two coming from tonight?'

'Nunya,' Khalil says, meaning none of your business. 'What you pull me over for?'

'Your taillight's broken.'

'So are you gon' give me a ticket or what?' Khalil asks.

'You know what? Get out the car, smart guy.'

'Man, just give me my ticket –'

'Get out the car! Hands up, where I can see them.'

Khalil gets out with his hands up. One-Fifteen yanks him by his arm and pins him against the back door.

I fight to find my voice. 'He didn't mean –'

'Hands on the dashboard!' the officer barks at me. 'Don't move!'

I do what he tells me, but my hands are shaking too much to be still.

He pats Khalil down. 'Okay, smart mouth, let's see what we find on you today.'

'You ain't gon' find nothing,' Khalil says.

One-Fifteen pats him down two more times. He turns up empty.

'Stay here,' he tells Khalil. 'And you.' He looks in the window at me. 'Don't move.'

I can't even nod.

The officer walks back to his patrol car.

POWER, FREEDOM AND CONTROL

My parents haven't raised me to fear the police, just to be smart around them. They told me it's not smart to move while a cop has his back to you.

Khalil does. He comes to his door.

It's not smart to make a sudden move.

Khalil does. He opens the driver's door.

'You okay, Starr –'

Pow!

One. Khalil's body jerks. Blood splatters from his back. He holds on to the door to keep himself upright.

Pow!

Two. Khalil gasps.

Pow!

Three. Khalil looks at me, stunned.

He falls to the ground.

I'm ten again, watching Natasha drop.

An earsplitting scream emerges from my gut, explodes in my throat, and uses every inch of me to be heard.

Instinct says don't move, but everything else says check on Khalil. I jump out the Impala and rush around to the other side. Khalil stares at the sky as if he hopes to see God. His mouth is open like he wants to scream. I scream loud enough for the both of us.

'No, no, no,' is all I can say, like I'm a year old and it's the only word I know. I'm not sure how I end up on the ground next to him. My mom once said that if someone gets shot, try to stop the bleeding. But there's so much blood. Too much blood.

'No, no, no.'

Khalil doesn't move. He doesn't utter a word. He doesn't even look at me. His body stiffens and he's gone. I hope he sees God.

Someone else screams.

I blink through my tears. Officer One-Fifteen yells at me, pointing the same gun he killed my friend with.

I put my hands up.

DIVERSE SHORTS

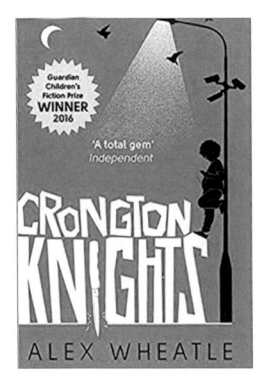

Crongton Knights, by Alex Wheatle

This extract comes from a novel about life on the fictional South Crongton council estate. The narrator, McKay, is walking with his older brother, Nesta, after they have been to the police station to report the theft of Nesta's bike. Nesta is normally in trouble with the police and would stay away from them, but he has been persuaded to turn over a new leaf by his girlfriend, Yvonne.

Connecting to the topic

Crongton Knights is part of the *Crongton* sequence. The other books written so far in the series are *Straight Outta Crongton* and *Liccle Bit*. The books have proved popular in part because they portray the lives of people who don't often feature in fiction: young, urban teenagers who speak in a distinctive dialect.

- Imagine you have been asked to write a novel based on the lives of young people in your school, or where you live. Write a paragraph or two, outlining the aspects of life that you would explore. If you like, you can come up with an outline for a story.

- Share your ideas round the class and discuss whether you think other readers would be interested in your ideas.

Connecting to the story

- How do you think Nesta's behaviour is portrayed in this extract? Was he provoked into acting as he did? Is there ever an excuse for this kind of behaviour? What should happen to him now? Write down your thoughts.

Connecting to the real world

In the extract you have just read, there seems to be a lot of distrust between people on the estate, particularly young people, and the police.

- Imagine a new character in *Crongton Knights*: a youth leader, who liaises between young people and the police. Script a meeting between the youth leader and a police chief, in which they discuss how to make life better for everyone on the South Crongton estate. The youth leader should mainly focus on young people, the police chief should focus on everyone else.

- Read out loud some of your scripts and use them as the basis for discussing how young people and the police can develop and maintain respectful relationships, even in difficult circumstances.

POWER, FREEDOM AND CONTROL

CRONGTON KNIGHTS

ALEX WHEATLE

Stop and Search

We walked back along the High Street. There were now six feds on patrol – three on either side. The Hot Rooster take-away was teasing my nostrils. Nesta was still jibber-jabbering away about Yvonne this and Yvonne that. It was funny. He hadn't said a fat zero to me about her before today. It sounds cold but I blocked him out.

A couple or so days ago Dad had bought a tray of chicken fillets that he had left in the fridge. I wanted to get back, slice and dice up a piece of prime rooster, spin some seasoning on it, chop up onions, peppers, garlic and stir-fry that mother with veg and a serious dose of Jamaican jerk. Yeah, I think there was a little bit of olive oil left to fry it in. I'd let it steam for a few minutes under some foil and get it smelling all sexy and ripe for sinking. And a pot of rice too, boiled up sweetly on the stove to go with it. Mmm. My mouth was watering big time.

'So, what do you think?' Nesta asked me as we headed towards South Crong ends.

'Think of what?' I said.

'Haven't you been listening to me, McKay? Yvonne, innit.'

'Yvonne,' I repeated. 'What about her?'

'What's a matter with you? I asked you what you think of her.'

'Oh, she seems cool,' I answered. 'But crush your balls! She has you under lock though! *Go to the fed station... Speak to your dad!*'

'No, she ain't,' Nesta argued. 'I just respect her.'

I killed another smirk.

We rolled towards the shop in the middle of our estate cos Nesta was thirsty – I hoped he would buy me a drink too. I was wondering if Nesta was gonna step back to our castle with me, when I saw flashing blue lights about a hundred metres away – not too far from the shop.

'Step it up, bruv,' Nesta told me. 'Something's going down.'

We hot-toed to the scene. A crowd had gathered on the pavement outside the store. A fed car was parked up and Mr Dagthorn, the forever stressed-out bald-headed owner of the place, was pointing this way and that, mauling the ears of two male feds. About thirty metres away, two other feds were dragging a hood-rat off towards their car, which they'd parked a little further along the road. Collie Vulture! His hands were cuffed behind his back. Curses spat from his mouth. His bike was abandoned on the pavement. I glanced at Nesta. He was shaking his head and spitting something dark under his breath. I spotted Boy from the Hills leaning against the shop door and bounced up to him. 'What's the score?' I asked.

'Collie jacked a bottle of tonic wine from the shop but when he jumped on his bike the feds appeared out of nowhere.'

I shook my head.

'Collie was raging. He'd promised Mr Dagthorn he'd pay him tomorrow,' Boy from the Hills added.

I rewound to earlier in the afternoon when Collie asked Yvonne for a fiver for collecting me from school. It was messed up how small dramas could turn into major blockbusters.

'I've banned him from coming in here but he's always stealing from my shop,' ranted Mr Dagthorn to the officers.

'Sweets, chocolate bars, chewing gum, porno mags – I'm sick and tired of young people robbing from me. Throw away the bloody key, I say!'

Collie heard what Mr Dagthorn said and wasted no time in biting back. 'Screw you, old man. I said I'd pay for the drink tomorrow and I would have!'

The feds tried to shove Collie into the back seat of their car. Collie put up nuff resistance. '*Get* in the car!' one of the feds ordered.

In trying to get away, Collie banged his head on the door handle. A red mark appeared across his eyebrow. Onlookers raged their disapproval. More people were starting to pay attention now; windows opened in the slabs above us. A council worker, wearing a yellow Day-Glo top, stopped sweeping the street and tuned in to the drama.

'Don't you *ever* enter my shop again,' yelled Mr Dagthorn. 'You'll probably even steal from the prison canteen!'

Someone threw a fat stone, hitting one of the fed cars on its bonnet. We all turned to see a hood-rat Usain-Bolting away from the scene towards Wareika Way.

POWER, FREEDOM AND CONTROL

The soles of his trainers were bright orange. I tried not to laugh, but it was well funny. The feds weren't exactly singing 'Always Look on the Bright Side of Life'. Poor Collie yelped and shrieked as they slam-dunked him hard through the car door. Nesta's expression switched.

Someone threw another stone, and blitzed the front window of Mr Dagthorn's shop. A nine or ten-year-old boy laughed as he burned off through the estate, a fed hot on his heels.

Boy from the Hills and I stepped away quickly, not wanting to get caught up in any trouble.

'Everyone *calm* down,' shouted an officer.

'You see what I have to put up with!' roared Mr Dagthorn, his hands now on his head. 'You see how much respect they have for me? Do I deserve this? If I wasn't here where would they go to get their milk for the morning? I'm just trying to make a living and *this* is how they treat me!'

Nesta approached the officers who had Collie. 'If I pay for the drink he jacked, will you let him go?'

'He's committed a crime,' a fed replied. 'We can't have everybody walking into shops and taking what they like.'

'It doesn't even cost three pound,' said Nesta. 'And Dagthorn charges fifty pence more than the supermarket – freaking t'ief! I'll pay for it and, trust me, after I spill to his sis he won't ever jack from the shop again.'

I wasn't sure if Nesta had three pound on him. My own funds were low – I only had twenty-seven pence blessing my pocket.

The fed shook his head and slammed the car door. The other officer climbed into the driver's seat and switched the ignition. Nesta slapped the window. Mr Dagthorn had stopped his ranting and was now watching my brother like everybody else.

'Nesta!' I called. He didn't hear me. The Kraken was about to be set loose. *Oh crap!*

'Can't you feds be on a freaking level?' Nesta raged, hammering the top of the fed car. 'Why arrest him for something that don't even cost three pound? Let him *go!* Nobody was hurt. He hasn't even touched the bottle. It can go back on the friggin' shelf.'

My heartbeat accelerated. The officer inside the car pushed the passenger door open. It smacked Nesta in the leg, nearly knocking him over. 'Why don't you move along!' ordered the fed to my brother. 'And go home!'

147

© ENGLISH & MEDIA CENTRE, 2018

I could feel Nesta's rage burst. Without hesitation he ran into the fed and headbutted him dead in the chest. The officer lost his balance and fell hard on to the ground.

Someone cheered from the pavement. A girl giggled hysterically. Even the road sweeper had a smile on his face. Others stared in disbelief.

'Nesta!' I shouted again.

The feds gathered round. Two of them grabbed my bro in a hard bear hug, almost strangling him, trying to put cuffs on him. Nesta wriggled this way and that, kicked and flailed. He managed to scratch a face or two, but he was overpowered.

Everyone around me cussed the feds. A voice inside me screamed, *Don't stand up there like a pussy! Help him! Help him!*

I started off to Nesta's aid, but Boy from the Hills barged me to the ground and said, 'McKay, keep your big self still.'

My right knee kissed the concrete.

'The feds are arresting my bro!'

'And how's your dad gonna feel when news beats him that not one but two of his boys are sinking oats in a fed cell?'

By the time I climbed to my feet, Nesta was being handcuffed. All struggle left him. His chest was heaving but he was weirdly calm. I think he was staring at me. His mouth was moving. I guessed at what he was saying. He wouldn't want me to tell Dad.

They shoved him into another car. Doors were slammed. Engines were revved. I watched as he sped away. He didn't look back. The road sweeper resumed sweeping.

POWER, FREEDOM AND CONTROL

1984, by George Orwell

Nineteen Eighty-Four is one of the best-known novels ever written. It is set in a brutal totalitarian regime, ruled by the symbolically named Big Brother. Under this regime, there are no elections and there is no law. Big Brother watches everything and controls everyone. The extract you are about to read comes from the very start of the novel.

Connecting to the topic

Nineteen Eighty-Four describes a 'surveillance state': the state tries to watch everything that each citizen does, in order to control them. Even though the United Kingdom is a democracy, some people still refer to it as a 'surveillance state'. This is because our movements can – and at times are – tracked to a degree that has never happened before. For example, CCTV cameras track people's movements, and we leave a 'digital footprint' when we use the internet, or mobile phone technology.

- In small groups discuss your responses to the following statements, before opening up the discussion to the class as a whole.

The principle of free speech should mean that anyone can say anything at any time and in any place.
The government should be allowed to look at your internet search history without seeking permission.
There are too many CCTV cameras in this country.

Connecting to the story

At the end of the extract you have just read, Winston Smith is about to write his first diary entry.

- In a pair, write a paragraph or two of this entry, trying to imagine Winston's feelings both about the world he lives in and about what he is doing.

- Listen to some examples of your diary entries round the class, then discuss how different Winston's experience of life is compared to the way people live in the United Kingdom today.

Connecting to the real world

- Have a go at writing a second diary entry, this one giving the thoughts and feelings Winston would have if he spent a day in the United Kingdom as it is now. You might like to focus on what he would think about the values of democracy and equality that you can find in the United Kingdom.

DIVERSE SHORTS

NINETEEN EIGHTY-FOUR

GEORGE ORWELL

Chapter I

It was a bright cold day in April, and the clocks were striking thirteen. Winston Smith, his chin nuzzled into his breast in an effort to escape the vile wind, slipped quickly through the glass doors of Victory Mansions, though not quickly enough to prevent a swirl of gritty dust from entering along with him.

The hallway smelt of boiled cabbage and old rag mats. At one end of it a coloured poster, too large for indoor display, had been tacked to the wall. It depicted simply an enormous face, more than a metre wide: the face of a man of about forty-five, with a heavy black moustache and ruggedly handsome features. Winston made for the stairs. It was no use trying the lift. Even at the best of times it was seldom working, and at present the electric current was cut off during daylight hours. It was part of the economy drive in preparation for Hate Week. The flat was seven flights up, and Winston, who was thirty-nine and had a varicose ulcer above his right ankle, went slowly, resting several times on the way. On each landing, opposite the lift shaft, the poster with the enormous face gazed from the wall. It was one of those pictures which are so contrived that the eyes follow you about when you move. BIG BROTHER IS WATCHING YOU, the caption beneath it ran.

Inside the flat a fruity voice was reading out a list of figures which had something to do with the production of pig-iron. The voice came from an oblong metal plaque like a dulled mirror which formed part of the surface of the right-hand wall. Winston turned a switch and the voice sank somewhat, though the words were still distinguishable. The instrument (the telescreen, it was called) could be dimmed, but there was no way of shutting it off completely. He moved over to the window: a smallish, frail figure, the meagreness of his body merely emphasised by the blue overalls which were the uniform of the Party. His hair was very fair, his face naturally sanguine, his skin roughened by coarse soap and blunt razor blades and the cold of the winter that had just ended.

Outside, even through the shut window-pane, the world looked cold. Down in the street little eddies of wind were whirling dust and torn paper into spirals,

POWER, FREEDOM AND CONTROL

and though the sun was shining and the sky a harsh blue, there seemed to be no colour in anything, except the posters that were plastered everywhere. The black moustachio'd face gazed down from every commanding corner. There was one on the house-front immediately opposite. BIG BROTHER IS WATCHING YOU, the caption said, while the dark eyes looked deep into Winston's own. Down at street level another poster, torn at one corner, flapped fitfully in the wind, alternately covering and uncovering the single word INGSOC. In the far distance a helicopter skimmed down between the roofs, hovered for an instant like a bluebottle, and darted away again with a curving flight. It was the police patrol, snooping into people's windows. The patrols did not matter, however. Only the Thought Police mattered.

Behind Winston's back the voice from the telescreen was still babbling away about pig-iron and the over-fulfilment of the Ninth Three-Year Plan. The telescreen received and transmitted simultaneously. Any sound that Winston made, above the level of a very low whisper, would be picked up by it; moreover, so long as he remained within the field of vision which the metal plaque commanded, he could be seen as well as heard. There was of course no way of knowing whether you were being watched at any given moment. How often, or on what system, the Thought Police plugged in on any individual wire was guesswork. It was even conceivable that they watched everybody all the time. But at any rate they could plug in your wire whenever they wanted to. You had to live – did live, from habit that became instinct – in the assumption that every sound you made was overheard, and, except in darkness, every movement scrutinised.

Winston kept his back turned to the telescreen. It was safer; though, as he well knew, even a back can be revealing. A kilometre away the Ministry of Truth, his place of work, towered vast and white above the grimy landscape. This, he thought with a sort of vague distaste – this was London, chief city of Airstrip One, itself the third most populous of the provinces of Oceania. He tried to squeeze out some childhood memory that should tell him whether London had always been quite like this. Were there always these vistas of rotting nineteenth-century houses, their sides shored up with baulks of timber, their windows patched with cardboard and their roofs with corrugated iron, their crazy garden walls sagging in all directions? And the bombed sites where the plaster dust swirled in the air and the willowherb straggled over the heaps of rubble; and the places where the bombs had cleared a larger patch and there had sprung up sordid colonies of wooden dwellings like chicken-houses? But it was no use, he could not remember: nothing remained of his childhood except a series of bright-lit tableaux, occurring against no background and mostly unintelligible.

DIVERSE SHORTS

The Ministry of Truth – Minitrue, in Newspeak – was startlingly different from any other object in sight. It was an enormous pyramidal structure of glittering white concrete, soaring up, terrace after terrace, three hundred metres into the air. From where Winston stood it was just possible to read, picked out on its white face in elegant lettering, the three slogans of the Party:

WAR IS PEACE

FREEDOM IS SLAVERY

IGNORANCE IS STRENGTH

The Ministry of Truth contained, it was said, three thousand rooms above ground level, and corresponding ramifications below. Scattered about London there were just three other buildings of similar appearance and size. So completely did they dwarf the surrounding architecture that from the roof of Victory Mansions you could see all four of them simultaneously. They were the homes of the four Ministries between which the entire apparatus of government was divided. The Ministry of Truth, which concerned itself with news, entertainment, education and the fine arts. The Ministry of Peace, which concerned itself with war. The Ministry of Love, which maintained law and order. And the Ministry of Plenty, which was responsible for economic affairs. Their names, in Newspeak: Minitrue, Minipax, Miniluv and Miniplenty.

The Ministry of Love was the really frightening one. There were no windows in it at all. Winston had never been inside the Ministry of Love, nor within half a kilometre of it. It was a place impossible to enter except on official business, and then only by penetrating through a maze of barbed-wire entanglements, steel doors and hidden machine-gun nests. Even the streets leading up to its outer barriers were roamed by gorilla-faced guards in black uniforms, armed with jointed truncheons.

Winston turned round abruptly. He had set his features into the expression of quiet optimism which it was advisable to wear when facing the telescreen. He crossed the room into the tiny kitchen. By leaving the Ministry at this time of day he had sacrificed his lunch in the canteen, and he was aware that there was no food in the kitchen except a hunk of dark-coloured bread which had got to be saved for tomorrow's breakfast. He took down from the shelf a bottle of colourless liquid with a plain white label marked VICTORY GIN. It gave off a sickly, oily smell, as of Chinese rice-spirit. Winston poured out nearly a teacupful, nerved himself for a shock, and gulped it down like a dose of medicine.

Instantly his face turned scarlet and the water ran out of his eyes. The stuff was like nitric acid, and moreover, in swallowing it one had the sensation of being

POWER, FREEDOM AND CONTROL

hit on the back of the head with a rubber club. The next moment, however, the burning in his belly died down and the world began to look more cheerful. He took a cigarette from a crumpled packet marked VICTORY CIGARETTES and incautiously held it upright, whereupon the tobacco fell out onto the floor. With the next he was more successful. He went back to the living room and sat down at a small table that stood to the left of the telescreen.

From the table drawer he took out a penholder, a bottle of ink and a thick, quarto-sized blank book with a red back and a marbled cover.

For some reason the telescreen in the living room was in an unusual position. Instead of being placed, as was normal, in the end wall, where it could command the whole room, it was in the longer wall, opposite the window. To one side of it there was a shallow alcove in which Winston was now sitting, and which, when the flats were built, had probably been intended to hold bookshelves. By sitting in the alcove, and keeping well back, Winston was able to remain outside the range of the telescreen, so far as sight went. He could be heard, of course, but so long as he stayed in his present position he could not be seen. It was partly the unusual geography of the room that had suggested to him the thing that he was now about to do.

But it had also been suggested by the book that he had just taken out of the drawer. It was a peculiarly beautiful book. Its smooth creamy paper, a little yellowed by age, was of a kind that had not been manufactured for at least forty years past. He could guess, however, that the book was much older than that. He had seen it lying in the window of a frowsy little junk-shop in a slummy quarter of the town (just what quarter he did not now remember) and had been stricken immediately by an overwhelming desire to possess it. Party members were supposed not to go into ordinary shops ('dealing on the free market', it was called), but the rule was not strictly kept, because there were various things such as shoelaces and razor blades which it was impossible to get hold of in any other way. He had given a quick glance up and down the street and then had slipped inside and bought the book for two dollars fifty. At the time he was not conscious of wanting it for any particular purpose. He had carried it guiltily home in his briefcase. Even with nothing written in it, it was a compromising possession.

The thing that he was about to do was to open a diary. This was not illegal (nothing was illegal, since there were no longer any laws), but if detected it was reasonably certain that it would be punished by death, or at least by twenty-five years in a forced-labour camp. Winston fitted a nib into the penholder and sucked it to get the grease off. The pen was an archaic instrument, seldom used even for signatures, and he had procured one, furtively and with some difficulty, simply because of a feeling that the beautiful creamy paper deserved to be written on with a real nib instead of being scratched with an ink-pencil. Actually he was not used to writing by hand. Apart from very short notes, it was usual to dictate everything into the speakwrite, which was of course impossible for his present purpose. He dipped the pen into the ink and then faltered for just a second. A tremor had gone through his bowels. To mark the paper was the decisive act. In small clumsy letters he wrote:

April 4th, 1984.

He sat back. A sense of complete helplessness had descended upon him. To begin with he did not know with any certainty that this was 1984. It must be round about that date, since he was fairly sure that his age was thirty-nine, and he believed that he had been born in 1944 to 1945; but it was never possible nowadays to pin down any date within a year or two. For whom, it suddenly occurred to him to wonder, was he writing this diary? For the future, for the unborn. His mind hovered for a moment round the doubtful date on the page, and then fetched up with a bump against the Newspeak word *doublethink*. For the first time the magnitude of what he had undertaken came home to him. How could you communicate with the future? It was of its nature impossible. Either the future would resemble the present, in which case it would not listen to him: or it would be different from it, and his predicament would be meaningless.

For some time he sat gazing stupidly at the paper. The telescreen had changed over to strident military music. It was curious that he seemed not merely to have lost the power of expressing himself, but even to have forgotten what it was that he had originally intended to say. For weeks past he had been making ready for this moment, and it had never crossed his mind that anything would be needed except courage. The actual writing would be easy. All he had to do was to transfer to paper the interminable restless monologue that had been running inside his head, literally for years. At this moment, however, even the monologue had dried up. Moreover his varicose ulcer had begun itching unbearably. He dared not scratch it, because if he did so it always became inflamed. The seconds were ticking by. He was conscious of nothing except the blankness of the page in front of him, the itching of the skin above his ankle, the blaring of the music, and a slight booziness caused by the gin.

Suddenly he began writing in sheer panic, only imperfectly aware of what he was setting down. His small but childish handwriting straggled up and down the page, shedding first its capital letters and finally even its full stops:

April 4th, 1984. Last night…

CRITICAL LITERACY QUESTIONS

Critical Literacy Questions

These questions have been developed to use with any or all of the stories and extracts in this anthology. They can also be applied to almost any other text. They are to help you develop your skills of *critical literacy*: this is a way of actively reading texts so that you can better understand how they are put together and the underlying messages that they contain.

There are nine sets of questions to match the different thematic categories explored in the anthology. You can select the set of questions that you think best matches a particular piece of writing within its category, or you can apply them across categories.

The questions are written to help you think deeply about texts, to challenge your initial responses, and to engage in the wider world. If you or your teacher want to print them off to use elsewhere, you can find copies by searching 'Diverse Shorts' at www.englishandmedia.co.uk/publications.

Freedom

Former US President, Franklin Roosevelt proposed four fundamental freedoms every person in the world should enjoy:

- Freedom of speech
- Freedom of religion/belief
- Freedom from fear
- Freedom from want.

- Thinking about the four freedoms above, consider:
  - In what ways are the characters in the story free/unfree?
  - Who in the story enjoys the most freedom? Why?
  - Who in the story has the least freedom? Why?
- What threatens the freedom of the characters in the story? Do these threats affect some characters more than others? Do the same threats exist for your own freedom?
- What, if anything, promotes or protects the freedom of the characters in the story? Is this true for you?
- Which people or organisations are responsible for promoting/protecting your freedom? Does having more freedom mean we have more responsibility? How is this shown in the story?
- Do you feel you have more/less freedom than the characters in the story? Why/why not?
- In the story, do any characters have to give up any personal freedom for the wellbeing of the community? Does this ever happen in real life? Is it a good thing?

DIVERSE SHORTS

Diversity and community

Thinking about the different communities represented in the story:

- Why do you think the author has chosen to write about these groups/communities?
- How are they represented? E.g. positively/negatively, strong/weak, tolerant/intolerant?
- Does the author choose to represent any groups/communities in the story which we don't often see/hear from in books, films etc.?
- Would everyone agree with the way the different people/groups/communities are represented?
- Are there any points of view lacking or not represented in the story which you think should be included? Why might the author not have included these views?
- Do you think the author might favour some groups/communities over others? How do you know? How might the story have an impact on the reader's thoughts or beliefs about certain groups/communities?
- How do the actions of different characters/groups in the story have an impact on the wellbeing of the different communities?
- Does the story contain any message about diversity and/or community? Do you agree with the message(s) in the story?

Justice

- What does this story make you think about the way the world works? Does the story suggest the author thinks the world is a place of justice and fairness or something else?
- What examples or events can we see in the story which connect to justice? Do you agree with how justice is represented in the story?
- What messages connected to justice does the story contain? Who might benefit if the message in the story is accepted? Who, if anyone, might be disadvantaged?
- What are the greatest threats to justice presented in the story? Do you think the same is true in the wider world? Do you agree with the way the author has tried to represent the world? Would anybody disagree? Why/why not?
- Are all the characters treated fairly in the story? Does the story encourage readers to challenge injustice? If so, how?
- How do the characters' choices and actions work to increase or reduce justice in their communities/the world?
- Would the world be any different if everybody read this story? If so, how? If not, why not?
- Would you like to live in the world described in the story? Does the story reflect your understanding of how the world works?

CRITICAL LITERACY QUESTIONS

Change and action

- Does the author think the world needs to change in some way? If so, how?
- Would everybody agree with the author?
- How do the actions and choices of the characters in the story have an impact on their lives and their communities? Do the characters' actions help to change the world for the better or worse?
- How might reading this story change the way a person thinks about:
    a. Themselves
    b. Other people
    c. Society/their community
    d. The wider world?
- Does the story make you think you need to change in some way? If so, how? If not, why not?
- Do you think the world would be a better place (even in a very small way) if everybody read this story? Why/why not?
- Does the story contain any ideas/suggestions/examples for how to change the world for the better?
- Does the story contain any messages about how we should/should not to act in society?
- How might people who have read the story work to change the world for the better?

Power and control

- Who in the story has the most power? How did they get this power/where does this power come from? Do the characters in the story use their power in a positive/negative way?
- Who in the story has the least power? Why don't they have much power? What would need to change for them to become more powerful?
- Who in the story has control/who doesn't have control? Where and/or how is this represented?
- How are power and control related in the story? Are the more powerful characters more in control (over their own thoughts and actions, over others in their community, of their place in society)?
- Does the amount of power/control the different characters have shift or change at all throughout the story? Why/how does this happen?
- What might the story teach us about power and control in the real world?
- Thinking about your own experiences, do you think the representation of power and/or control in the story is realistic?

DIVERSE SHORTS

Identity

- How are different identities, e.g. gender, race, class etc. represented in the story? To what extent does the author present the different characters' identities as complex and multiple, i.e. consisting of many parts? Are some characters identities more complex than others? How does the author represent this?
- Do you agree with the way different identities in the story are represented?
- Are any parts of your identity represented in the story/ by the characters? Are you happy with this representation?
- What factors affect and shape the characters' identities in the story? Does the author present identity as something we are in control of or something that is decided for us?
- How are different voices presented in the story? Are any voices stronger/ weaker than others? What makes them strong/ weak?
- Is there a voice/ identity missing from the story? If you could add this voice into the story, what would it say?
- Do you think everybody would read and respond to the story in the same way? How might people's identities affect how they feel about the story?
- What, if anything, might the story suggest to the reader about the author's own identity?

Tolerance, rights and respect

- To what extent is the society represented in the story 'tolerant and respectful'? Is the story a realistic depiction of society?
- Does anything happen in the story which you don't agree with but **would** tolerate? Should we have to tolerate things we don't agree with? Why/why not?
- Are there any actions/events/beliefs in the story which you think **should not be tolerated**? Why not? How do the characters in the story respond to such events? Do you agree with their response?
- Are there any views or beliefs represented in the story which you don't agree with? Are these views held by many in wider society? Is it a bad thing when people disagree in society?
- Are there any characters, groups or communities who are treated disrespectfully in the story? Where do we see this? Does this reflect real life?
- To what extent do you think the characters in the story demonstrate respect for:
    a. each other's and their rights
    b. their communities
    c. rules, laws and institutions of society (e.g. police, government etc.).
- What lessons, if any, does the story contain about how we ought to treat each other? Do you agree with these messages?

CRITICAL LITERACY QUESTIONS

Democracy

- Think of some important features of a democratic society (e.g. freedom of speech). To what extent is the society presented in the story a 'democratic' society? How do we know?
- To what extent do the different characters in the story feel happy/content with the world? How does the author represent their feelings? Do you identify with any of these ideas/feelings?
- To what extent are the characters in the story able to express their views/ideas/beliefs hopes/frustrations effectively?
- Are some characters in the story more able to communicate their views/ideas/beliefs etc. than others? What enables them to do this?
- Should people ever be stopped from expressing their views/beliefs?
- Within a democracy, what methods can we use to communicate our views/beliefs responsibly and effectively? Do we see any of these in the story? Is there a positive outcome?
- Who/what might stop characters in the story from expressing their views and beliefs? Does the same thing happen in our society?
- Do the views, actions and choices of the characters reflect the ways in which people think and act in the real world? If so, how? If not, how is it different?

Equality and responsibility

- Are there any issues/themes in the story connected to either rights, equality or both?
- In the story, can you see any instances of people:
    - Claiming their rights
    - Protecting/promoting the rights of others
    - Having rights denied or restricted
    - Denying the rights of others?
- How is this shown? Is it ever necessary to limit or restrict someone's rights? Why/not?
- Where can inequality be seen in the story? What form(s) does it take? Is inequality ever desirable in society? Why/not?
- In the story, who/what are the greatest threats to equality? How do we see this?
- In the story, who/what, works to promote equality? How does this happen? In your opinion, does this reflect reality?
- Thinking about your own experiences of equality/inequality, does the story match your own understanding of how the world works? Is this a good thing?
- What would need to change in the story to increase the equality for the characters? Would this make it a better or worse story?
- How would reading this story influence the way people think about equality and/or rights in society?

DIVERSE SHORTS